COLOR BLOCK
QUILT MAKING

COLOR BLOCK
QUILT MAKING

12 Quick-and-Easy Statement Pieces to Decorate Your Space

ELIZABETH CHAPPELL

Landauer Publishing

Dedicated to all the quilters
(even those who don't know
they are one yet)

Color Block Quilt Making

Landauer Publishing, www.landauerpub.com, is an imprint of Fox Chapel Publishing Company, Inc.

Copyright 2022 by Elizabeth Chappell and Fox Chapel Publishing Company, Inc., 903 Square Street, Mount Joy, PA 17552.

Project Team
Editor: Hayley DeBerard
Designer: Wendy Reynolds
Proofreader and Indexer: Jean Bissell
Photographer: Tyan Jacox
Paintings on pages 12 and 13 by Sarah Nielsen

Images from www.Shutterstock.com:
3DJustincase (cover, 27), Jafara (69)

ISBN 978-1-947163-83-6

Library of Congress Control Number: 2021947085

We are always looking for talented authors. To submit an idea, please send a brief inquiry to acquisitions@foxchapelpublishing.com.

Printed in China
24 23 22 21 2 4 6 8 10 9 7 5 3 1

Contents

52

68

78

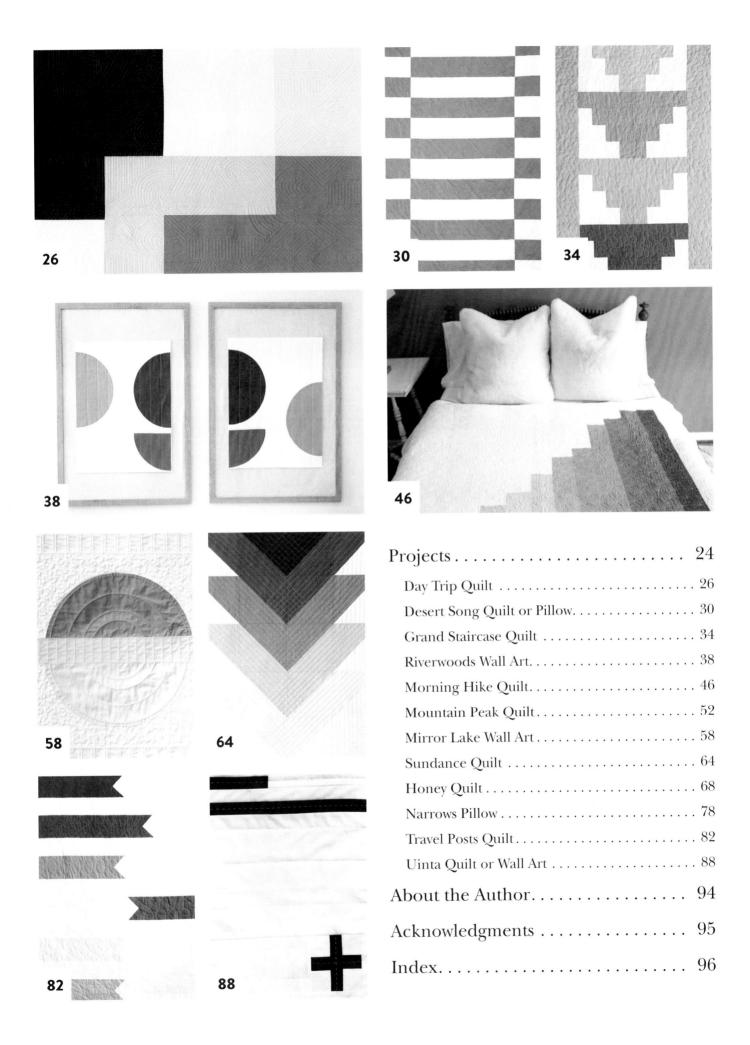

Projects 24

Introduction

I still can't believe that I am a quilter. Even though I grew up in a home where my mom was an award-winning quilter, it never felt like my thing. That was until I went to Quilt Market in Houston and got a glimpse of the fabrics, quilts, designs, and people that really excited me. I saw that quilting wasn't just for one demographic. The different ways fabrics were used as well as the different designs really spoke to all ages and people, myself included. Quilting became a lot cooler to me once I saw all the booths and ways people used fabrics as Quilt Market.

After getting a glimpse of modern quilting, I knew there was a place for me in the quilting world. Since 2015 I have been quilting, writing patterns, bringing quilters together with the Quilters Candy Membership, and more recently teaching others how to write and sell their own quilt patterns. The part of quilting that speaks to me the most is designing different quilts and choosing the fabrics to use. I love to see how different designs look when you combine and use different fabrics.

My typical quilt style is more block based, adding a modern twist to traditional quilts. When I was invited to make a color block quilt, I jumped at the chance. I wanted to push myself creatively. I wanted to try these truly modern designs that have more negative space than my typical quilts, are not block based, and focus on color as the number one feature. I was also excited because color block quilts fit my home style décor, so this was a chance for me to really mesh my home and my quilting designs in a way I hadn't before. Each design in this book can be used to enhance your surroundings with a modern color block project, either as a pillow, wall art, or a quilt.

I hope you enjoy the photos that show how you can use these quilts to decorate your space. You can use colors that fit your décor and style or try something new to add a little pop to your space.

So who is this book for…?
This book is for the artists and creators of the world. This is a book for those who may not know they are quilters yet, and for those who already know they are. As I mentioned, I didn't think quilting was for me until I went to Quilt Market. I don't know how else to describe it but magical, when I discovered the world of fabrics and quilting. I realized that quilting is an art form just like any other. Just as I have found a creative outlet in combining fabrics to create art, I am thrilled with the idea of others doing the same.

This book is for the creative who wants to make something with their own two hands. For those who want to create something that will last longer than they will, something that can be used now and passed down for generations. I am excited for you to create something uniquely you with the patterns you find in this book.

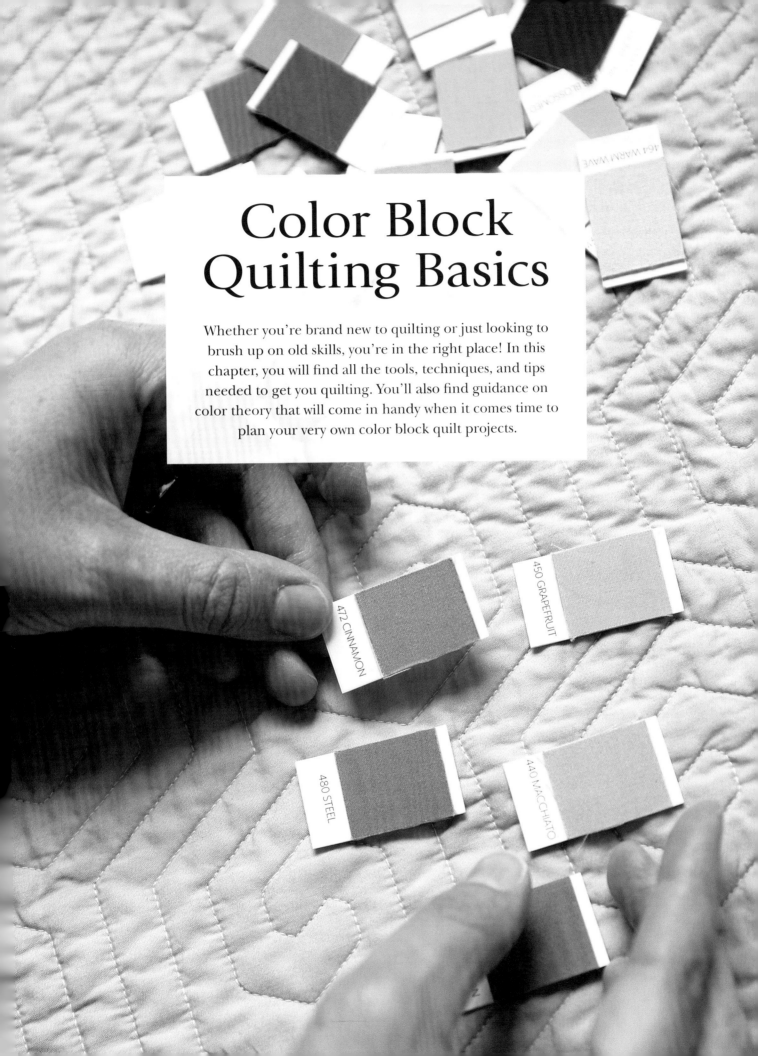

Color Block Quilting Basics

Whether you're brand new to quilting or just looking to brush up on old skills, you're in the right place! In this chapter, you will find all the tools, techniques, and tips needed to get you quilting. You'll also find guidance on color theory that will come in handy when it comes time to plan your very own color block quilt projects.

TOOLS AND SUPPLIES

SEWING MACHINE

I won't go much into detail about sewing machines as there are many options available, and virtually all of them will get the job done. If you're just starting out, you won't need anything fancy, so long as it sews straight, can switch feet, and is in good working condition! Whatever machine you have, I suggest making sure you feel comfortable threading and using it before getting started on larger projects.

QUILTING NEEDLES

There are many options for sewing machine needles; however, I like to use universal sewing machine needles as they are easily accessible and hold up well while quilting. It's best to use a new needle with each new project you start, as prolonged sewing dulls your needle and can cause damage to your fabric and machine.

PRESSER FOOT

Throughout all the projects in this book, you will be working with a ¼" (*0.5cm*) seam allowance. One of the easiest ways to maintain a consistent seam is to use a ¼" (*0.5cm*) presser foot. Keep in mind that some feet maintain this measurement when the needle is centered and the seam is sewn along the outer edge of the foot, while others have a small metal guide to move your fabric along when you are sewing a seam. Some machines even come with a dedicated ¼" (*0.5cm*) so check your machine before going out to buy one!

WALKING FOOT

If you plan to quilt your own quilts and projects, a walking foot comes in handy whenever you move three or more layers through your sewing machine. A walking foot has small ridges, or "feed dogs," on top of the foot that move in tandem with the feed dogs under the throat plate of your machine. Layers move through the machine at the same rate, preventing bunching or puckers.

THREAD

Choosing a good quilting thread helps avoid headaches as you sew, as it can help avoid snapping or shredding, as well as lint build-up in your machine. I use 50 weight 100% cotton thread, and it's my favorite. I always sew with white thread because it's the most comfortable for me, but you can use any color you like. When piecing, the hope is that no one sees your thread, so the color you use doesn't really matter. When you are quilting and sewing on your binding, you will want to make sure to use a thread that compliments the colors in your quilt or is that same color as the fabric in your quilt. I usually use white, as I mentioned. To me, white is a neutral color thread that doesn't stand out too much, so that's what I tend to use. But again, feel free to try different colors if that is something you want o experiment with.

ROTARY CUTTER

A rotary cutter is a handy tool used to cut your fabrics quickly. I recommend using a 45mm size rotary cutter. When you notice your rotary cutter getting stuck or not cutting all the way through your fabric, it's time to replace the circular blade. I keep at least two extra rotary cutter blades on hand at all times, as it's nice to have a sharp new blade ready to replace the dull one.

SELF-HEALING CUTTING MAT

If you use a rotary cutter, you will need a safe surface to cut on; self-healing mats are made for this. I recommend getting one that measures 24" x 36" (*61cm x 91.4cm*).

QUILTING RULERS

To cut your fabric accurately, you will need a quilting ruler. These rulers are made of clear acrylic so that you can see your fabric through them. I love Creative Grids® rulers and recommend getting a 6½" x 24½" (*16.5cm x 62.2cm*) rectangular ruler, and a 6½" x 6½" (*16.5cm x 16.5cm*) square ruler. These two sizes are what I use 90% of the time.

SCISSORS

Having a nice, small pair of scissors comes in handy when you trim threads and work on your projects.

PINS

The more pins you use while quilting, the more accurate your quilt will be in the end. I love using long, thin pins. The pins I use are Tulip brand, and they are so thin that they bend easily. This is helpful when I want my pin in an exact spot to nest my seams together. My pins bend easily to be in just the right place. But really, any good pin will do the trick! The main thing is to have your pins close at hand when you're ready to secure your fabrics together, as they will hold everything in place as you sew.

SEAM RIPPER

As much as we like to think we won't need a seam ripper, we all do at some point. Whenever there's a happy accident (a.k.a. a sewing mistake), you'll want one to help reopen seams and unpick stitches.

IRON

It is crucial to press your seams with an iron when sewing and quilting to ensure your quilt lays perfectly flat. I also recommend ironing your fabric before cutting it to make sure your cuts are accurate.
DO NOT use steam, just a dry, hot iron, and always use an ironing mat under your fabric.

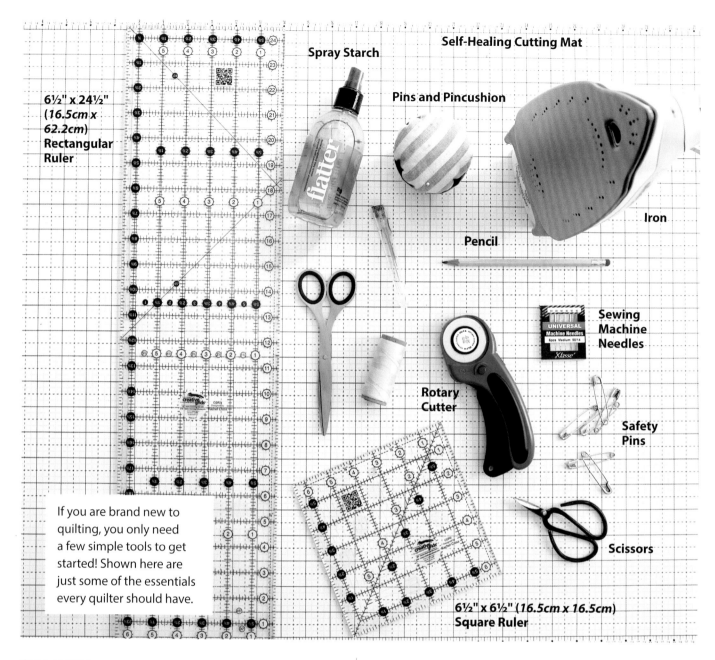

6½" x 24½" (16.5cm x 62.2cm) Rectangular Ruler

Spray Starch

Self-Healing Cutting Mat

Pins and Pincushion

Iron

Pencil

Sewing Machine Needles

Rotary Cutter

Safety Pins

Scissors

6½" x 6½" (16.5cm x 16.5cm) Square Ruler

If you are brand new to quilting, you only need a few simple tools to get started! Shown here are just some of the essentials every quilter should have.

STARCH

I love using starch or fabric spray when I quilt. I starch my fabric before I start cutting so that all of my piecing is accurate. I use both Soak Flatter Starch™ and Faultless®.

PAINTER'S OR MASKING TAPE

I know, odd. But you will be glad you have some when it comes to basting your quilt.

QUILTING COTTON

Not all fabrics are created equal. Even if a fabric is 100% cotton, I recommend using quilters cotton. This fabric is woven with a higher thread count, holds its shape better, and is usually softer. When it comes to choosing fabric colors, sometimes you'll want to create a quilt just as you see it, while other times you'll want to pick your own fabrics. Using the color theory lesson on page 12, you can feel confident in picking fabrics you like that work together.

BATTING

Batting is the insulating layer of a quilt. It goes in the middle of the quilt backing and top. It can be made of many different materials, but bamboo, cotton, polyester, and wool are the most common. The type of batting you use will affect how much quilting you'll need to do, so be sure to check with your batting manufacturer's recommendations on the packaging to see how far apart the quilting lines should be. Ultimately, the type of batting you use is a personal preference, depending on how you want your finished quilt to look and feel. I use wool batting and 100% natural cotton batting.

QUILTING TERMS AND ABBREVIATIONS

If you are new to quilting, you might be unfamiliar with some of the common quilting terms and abbreviations. Use this guide as a reference if you come across a word you don't know.

BACKING: The fabric used for the back of a quilt. Plan to have your backing fabric at least 8" (*20.3cm*) longer and wider than your finished quilt top. This will allow for a 4" (*10.2cm*) overhang on all sides.

FAT EIGHTH (F8): An eighth yard of fabric that measures 9" x 22" (*22.9cm x 55.9cm*).

FAT QUARTER (FQ): A quarter yard of fabric that measures 18" x 22" (*45.7cm x 55.9cm*).

FLYING GEESE: Rectangular quilting components with a peaked triangle at its center and small triangles flanking opposite peak ends.

LONGARM QUILTING: When a longarm sewing machine is used for quilting a quilt top. These expensive computerized machines can be programmed to quilt different designs for you on your finished quilt. Longarm machines are available to rent and use in craft stores to finish your quilts yourself, or professional longarm quilters can be hired to finish your quilts for you.

QUILT BLOCK: The combined pieced fabrics. Usually, an entire quilt top is made of smaller quilt blocks.

QUILT SANDWICH: The three layers (backing, batting, and quilt top) needed to make a finished quilt.

QUILT TOP: The top layer of a quilt made of pieced together fabrics. This is only part of a completed quilt, which also includes batting and a backing.

RIGHT SIDES TOGETHER (RST): When fabrics are placed front sides together, or the design or prints are faced together and touching.

SEAM ALLOWANCE: The distance between where you are sewing and the edge of your fabric. This book calls for you to use a ¼" (*0.5cm*) seam allowance throughout.

SELVAGE: The edge of the fabric where the threads are densely woven to prevent fraying. Selvage usually has the name of the fabric, the designer, and the manufacturer on it. You will want to cut the selvage off and make sure it's not used in your quilt.

SUBCUTTING (SUBCUT): When you cut a larger piece of fabric and then cut it into smaller pieces.

WIDTH OF FABRIC (WOF): The measurement of a fabric from selvage to selvage. This book assumes a useable WOF of 42" (*106.7cm*).

WRONG SIDES TOGETHER (WST): When fabrics are facing back sides together.

CHOOSING FABRICS USING COLOR THEORY

Picking fabric for a project can be overwhelming. Will it look good? Do the colors go together well? This is especially important when planning your color block quilts where the design is heavily influenced by color. While there is no "right" or "wrong" when it comes to selecting fabric colors, understanding the basics of color theory can help you create modern and balanced color block designs.

COLOR THEORY BASICS

Color Theory is the science behind why certain colors look good together. Open up any beginning art or design textbook, and you're sure to come across a color wheel, which maps the entire spectrum of colors. Color theory, as related to the color wheel, acts as a guide to understanding the mixing of colors and why some groupings appear more harmonious than others.

PRIMARY COLORS

The three primary colors that create every other color.

SECONDARY COLORS

Colors made by mixing two of the primary colors.

TERTIARY COLORS

Colors made by mixing one primary color with a secondary color.

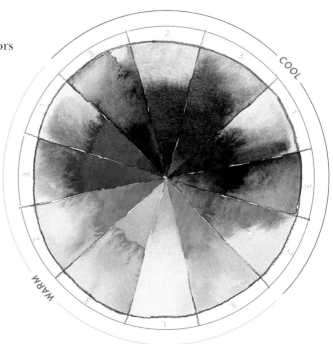

A color wheel can help you choose and group colors while planning your quilt.

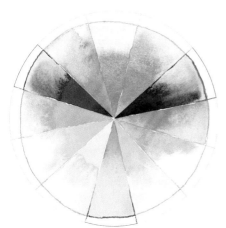

PRIMARY COLORS
Red, blue, yellow

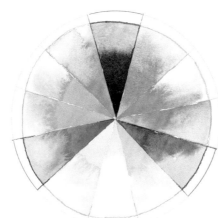

SECONDARY COLORS
Orange, purple, green

TERTIARY COLORS
Red-violet, blue-violet, blue-green, yellow-green, yellow-orange, red-orange

PICKING COLORS THAT LOOK GOOD TOGETHER

From the color wheel, you can find colors that look good together in the following ways:

MONOCHROMATIC

Pick a color on the color wheel, then utilize its shades or tints.

ANALOGOUS COLORS

Pick any three colors next to each other on the color wheel. TIP: avoid combining warm and cool colors.

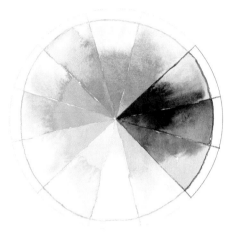

COMPLEMENTARY COLORS

Pick any two colors that are opposite of each other on the color wheel.

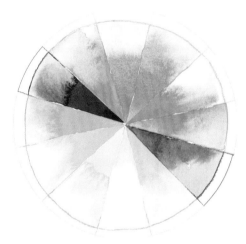

SPLIT COMPLEMENTARY COLORS

Pick one color on the wheel, then go directly across from it and choose the two neighboring colors.

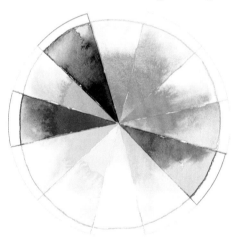

TRIADIC COLORS

Pick any three colors that are equally apart on the color wheel.

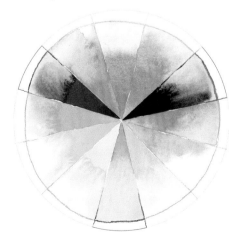

TETRADIC COLORS

Pick two pairs of complementary colors, all equal distance from each other on the color wheel.

DESIGNING YOUR OWN QUILTS

When it comes to planning for your finished projects, a little preliminary color-play goes a long way. Below are a few examples of how changing the colors of fabrics used for the quilts in this book can create completely different and personalized décor that matches your style.

The Day Trip quilt (page 26), as shown, utilizes triadic colors to create a bold, blocky look. However, switching to muted complementary or analogous colors would make for an exciting choice.

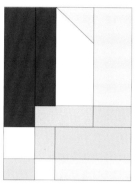

Colors used in the book

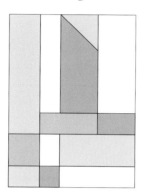
Analogous colors

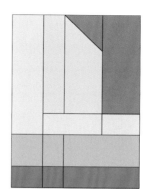
Complementary colors

The Desert Song design (page 30) makes for a beautiful monochromatic quilt, or you can use punchy split complementary or even tetradic colors in random order to add even more visual interest and movement to this graphic design.

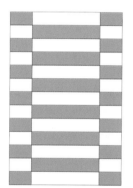
Colors used in the book

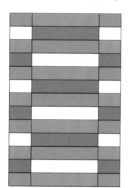
Split analogous colors

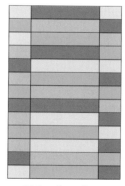
Tetradic colors

The Grand Staircase quilt (page 34) uses a tetradic color scheme but using a monochromatic or complementary palettes in innovative ways can give the design a completely different look!

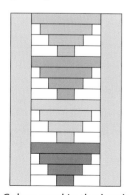
Colors used in the book

Analogous colors

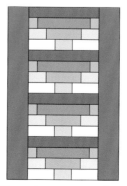
Complementary colors

TIP

Trace the finished quilt diagrams at the end of each pattern's instructions onto blank paper to use as coloring pages that you can use to help visualize your design!

CUTTING FABRIC

Each of the projects in this book will begin by telling you how much fabric you will need and how you need to cut it to prepare for piecing. For best cutting results, make sure to press your fabric before measuring and cutting to ensure that if shrinkage occurs, it happens before you cut pieces to size. Using starch or fabric spray while pressing can also help to flatten the fabric further.

Once your fabric is ready, gather your quilting ruler, cutting mat, and rotary cutter. Place your cutting mat on a flat, stable, waist-high surface and lay your fabric flat on top of the mat. Place your clear quilting ruler over the fabric, aligning the edge over where you'd like to cut. Remember that the assumed WOF in this book is 42" (*106.7cm*). If your fabric is wider than this, you will need to cut it down to size. Make sure to **double-check your measurements before cutting**! Holding your rotary cutter in your dominant hand and your ruler in place with your non-dominant hand, run the blade along the edge of the ruler to cut the fabric. Always **cut away from your body** to avoid injury.

TIP

Make sure to read through all of the pattern instructions before you begin.

Make sure to always cut away from yourself while using a rotary tool to cut fabric.

PIECING

Often mistaken for quilting, piecing is when you sew all of the cut pieces of fabric together, and each pattern in this book will outline exactly how to piece together your quilt top. Here are some helpful tips to remember while piecing:

- Pin before you sew. The more pins you use, the better chances you have at keeping everything together and straight.

- Remember seam allowance. Using a ¼" (0.5cm) presser foot will help you get a consistent and accurate seam allowance. If you do not have a ¼" (0.5cm) presser foot, align the needle on your machine on the quarter-inch (0.5cm) line of a ruler. Then, take a piece of tape and lay it against the edge of the ruler, pressing the tape down on the throat of your machine. Use the edge of the tape as your ¼" (0.5cm) guide.

- REMOVE PINS as you sew. Make sure to pull any pins before your sewing machine needle can sew over them, as this can break both the pin and the sewing machine needle. It can even cause the broken ends of the pin or needle to go flying (in some cases into your eye), so be very careful to avoid this!

The fabric triangles shown have been pieced together into a singular block by sewing them together along the long edges of the triangles.

PRESSING

Even if you're brand new to quilting, chances are you've probably used an iron at least once for household chores. Don't be fooled though; this is not the same action as ironing a shirt! In regular ironing, you place the iron on the fabric and move it from side to side. With quilting, it's important not to use your iron like this as this can warp your fabric and lead to a wonky quilt. Instead, **press your fabric** by placing your iron straight down on the fabric and lifting it straight back up, making sure **NOT** to move it from side to side.

Pressing your seams as you piece is critical as it makes for a better-finished quilt top. You can press seams in one of two ways:

1. Press the seams to one side. This means that when you press your seam, both sides of the fabric on either side of the seam should be pressed flat in the indicated direction.

2. Press seams open. This means that when you press your seam, the fabric on either side of the seam should be pressed flat in opposite directions.

Each project in this book includes directions for pressing while piecing. These pressing directions were thoughtfully written to create seams that best work for that pattern, so be sure to note which direction and way you are pressing.

BASTING

Once all the pieces of your quilt sandwich are ready, basting is needed to hold everything together in preparation for quilting. You can choose between pin basting or spray basting; however, I recommend pin basting if you are sensitive to fumes or scents. To *spray baste* your quilt:

1. Lay your quilt backing on a flat surface (I normally choose a hard floor) with the right side facing the floor. I usually use tape to secure the sides down so they don't move. Place your batting on top and center it with the backing. Smooth it out.

2. Lift half of the batting and spray the quilt backing (the wrong side that's facing up) with spray baste. Lower the batting back down, moving from the center out. Then, lift the other half of the batting and spray the quilt backing (the wrong side facing up) with spray baste. Lower the batting back down, moving from the center out.

3. Place your quilt top face up on top of the batting. I usually pull out an iron at this point and iron it out to make sure it's smooth and flat.

4. Lift half of the quilt top and spray the batting, repeating the same spraying pattern as in step 2. Iron the quilt top to flatten and seal the spray baste, moving from the center out.

To *pin baste*, layer the quilt sandwich the same as with spray basting, securing with safety pins, placing them 3"–4" (*7.6cm–10.2cm*) apart. Make sure the pins get all three layers of your quilt sandwich.

SUPPLIES

- 2" (*5cm*) safety pins for pin basting
- Spray baste if spray basting
- Painters, masking, or duct tape

Pin basting offers a fume-free alternative to basting.

QUILTING

Quilting is what holds your quilt sandwich together permanently. But it can also enhance the beauty of your quilt. There are two main ways to quilt. You can quilt on your own sewing machine or use (or hire) a longarm quilting machine. If you hire someone to longarm quilt for you, you won't have to worry about the next steps.

SUPPLIES

- Walking Foot: Sewing through all three layers of fabric on your machine is a lot! A walking foot helps grab all three layers and move them evenly through your sewing machine.
- Quilting Needle: Consider changing your sewing machine needle to a topstitch 80. It's a great all-purpose quilting needle.

QUILTING ON A SEWING MACHINE

When you are learning how to quilt, I recommend keeping quilting as simple as possible. For this book, we'll be stitching in the ditch, which means quilting on or as close as possible on your piecing seams. This technique makes for almost invisible stitching on the top of the quilt; however, the stitches add depth where they compress the quilt batting and are completely visible on the back of the quilt. As you gain more confidence and experience, feel free to experiment with more elaborate quilting designs on your color block quilts!

HIRING A LONG ARM QUILTER

After spending so much time on making your quilt top, deciding on a good long arm quilter can feel daunting. I have used several long arm quilters in the past, and all of them have been recommendations from someone I knew. I always suggest looking at previous work a long arm quilter has done. It's ideal if you know someone personally who can share their experience with a long arm quilter. Things to look for are what designs in quilting a long armer offers. You want to make sure they can do a quilting design that you like. You will want to know how soon you can expect to get your quilt back. You will also want to know what you will pay. And most important, you want to know that they do a good job and will take care of your quilt.

1. Start by looking to see which side of the seam is a bit higher—this is the side that the seam allowance was pressed toward. You want stitches to fall on the other, lower side of the line. Then, drop your sewing machine's needle where fabrics meet at a seam.

2. Stitch along the seam line, pulling the fabrics apart slightly on both sides of the seam as you sew. Sew to the end of the seam on the quilt top. It's fine if your seams are not completely consistent—just try to stitch a smooth, straight line, even though the stitches may end up on top of a seam allowance.

3. Depending on the size of your quilt, you may need to sew additional lines in other areas, away from the seams. Read the instructions that came with your quilt batting to determine the minimum distance apart that stitches must be sewn to keep the batting intact when the quilt is used and when you launder the quilt.

4. When you're done quilting your quilt, take it to your cutting table, and using a ruler and rotary cutter, square up your quilt top. Then, carefully trim your quilt sandwich so all excess backing and batting are removed. At this point, all that's left is adding the quilt binding.

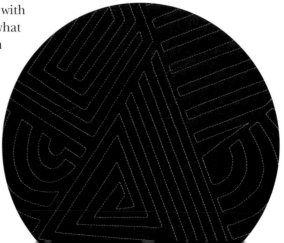

You can hire professional longarm quilters to quilt intricate patterns on your work like those used on the Day Trip quilt (page 26).

BINDING

The quilt binding is the border of your quilt. I consider it like a picture frame as it frames the quilt and holds the edges of your three-layer quilt sandwich together.

MAKING A BINDING STRIP

1. Make one continuous binding strip by placing two strips at right angles with ½" (*1.5cm*) overlapping. Mark a diagonal line from the top left corner to the bottom right.

2. Make sure to pin the pieces in place, and then stitch along your marked line.

3. Trim the corner outside of the sewn line.

4. Press the sewn seam open.

5. Then press the entire strip in half lengthwise with wrong sides together.

ATTACHING BINDING

1. Starting in the middle of one side of your quilt top, line up the raw, open edges of the binding with the raw, open edges of your quilt top.

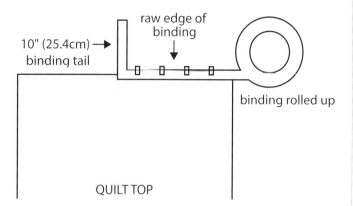

2. Leaving a 10" (*25.4cm*) tail of binding, use a ¼" (*0.5cm*) seam to sew the binding to the quilt top. When you get to the corner of your quilt, stop sewing ¼" (*0.5cm*) away from the edge of your quilt. Backstitch to secure your sewing.

3. Fold the binding upward to make a 90-degree angle. Crease the binding and fold it down to run along the next side of your quilt, raw open edges still aligned.

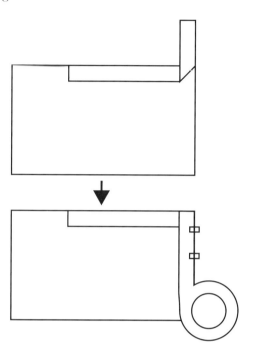

Add your binding strip to your unfinished project by first lining up the raw, open edges of the binding with the raw, open edges of your quilt top.

4. Start sewing ¼" (*0.5cm*) away from the corner of your quilt again. Continue until you get to the next corner of your quilt, and then repeat these steps.

5. When you get back to where your 10" (*25.4cm*) binding tail is, leave 10" (*25.4cm*) of the unbound quilt top. Bring your two ends (the beginning and the end) of your quilt binding together so they meet. There will be extra binding on both sides. Where the two ends of the binding meet, fold the binding back and finger press or press with your iron so there is a crease mark. The dashed lines show where binding has been sewn.

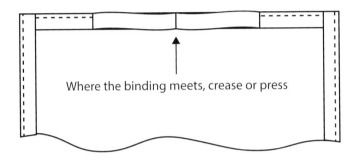

Where the binding meets, crease or press

6. Open the binding and place the beginning and end pieces of the binding RST. Sew exactly on the creased line.

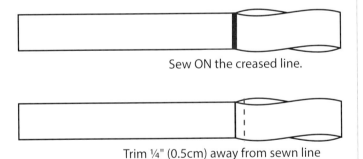

Sew ON the creased line.

Trim ¼" (0.5cm) away from sewn line

7. Trim ¼" (*0.5cm*) away from the sewn line. Before you trim, open your binding and make sure it lays flat and isn't too short or too long. If it isn't the right length, make adjustments as needed.

8. Once the binding has been trimmed, fold the binding back in half, and sew the rest of the binding to the quilt with the ¼" (*0.5cm*) seam allowance. Take your quilt with the binding sewn on the front to your iron. Fold the binding back toward the back of your quilt. I like to iron the binding at this point because it makes it SO much easier to sew. You won't be tugging and struggling to keep the binding in place.

9. Clip your binding to the back of the quilt and sew the binding to the back of your quilt. Again, use a ¼" (*0.5cm*) seam and a walking foot. Go slowly.

10. When you get to a corner, stop 6" (*15.2cm*) away from the corner. Fold your corner to be a mitered corner. To do this, fold one side of the binding down, then fold the other side over. Pin the corner. With the corner pinned, you can continue sewing until you get to the corner. Then, leaving your needle down, turn your quilt and start sewing down the other side. Repeat these steps for each corner.

MAKING A PILLOW

To make a pillow, you will first want to quilt your finished project. Follow the same steps as you would for normal quilting, but do not add the quilt binding.

1. Take your two pieces of pillow backing found in your pattern instructions under MATERIALS. Lay your backing fabrics together on top of your finished quilted project. Look to see how the two overlapping fabrics will lay and fit on your quilted project.

These are the sides of the backing that overlap. Make sure this is at least a 4" (10.2cm) overlap. Mark with a pin.

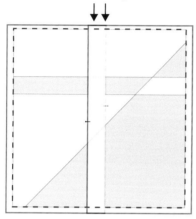

2. Make finished seams for the sides of your backing fabric that overlap by putting a pin on the edges of your backing fabric that will be the open, overlapping openings. Fold the pinned edges ½" (*1.5cm*), then fold again ½" (*1.5cm*). Press with an iron.

Fold the pinned edge in ½" (1.5cm), then ½" (1.5cm) again. Press with iron.

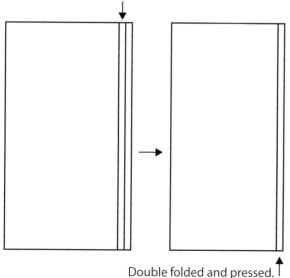

Double folded and pressed.

3. Topstitch as close to the edge of the fold as possible on both pieces of fabric. Be sure to backstitch at the beginning and end of your sewing to secure.

Topstitch as close to fold as possible.

4. Layer RST your quilted top and the two backing pieces of fabric. Make sure the backing pieces of fabric are overlapping with the sewn edges in the center. Pin all edges in place. Using a ¼" (*0.5cm*) seam, sew around the entire pillow.

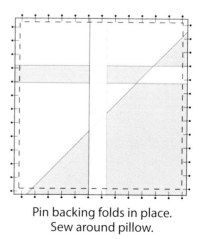

Pin backing folds in place. Sew around pillow.

5. Turn the pillowcase inside out and add the pillow insert.

An example of a finished Narrows pillow (page 78).

Projects

DAY TRIP

Day Trip represents, to me, the very definition of a "color block quilt",
as it's made entirely of big, blocks of color! I knew I needed to include a pattern
that featured big, funky shapes that allowed for bold color play. It's an ideal pattern
for using the color theory lessons on pages 12–14 and trying out different fabrics
and color combinations. It's also a breeze to piece and finish, even for
newbie quilters, while still resulting in a stunning final piece.

MATERIALS

*Yardage is based on 42"
(106.7cm)–wide fabric.*

- 1 yard (*91.4cm*) in Fabric A
  (navy blue)
- ⅜ yard (*34.3cm*) in Fabric B
  (light blue)
- ¾ yard (*68.6cm*) in Fabric C (orange)
- 1¼ yards (*114.3cm*) in Fabric D
  (pale pink)
- 1 yard (*91.4cm*) in Fabric E (white)
- 3¼ yards (*297.2cm*) of fabric
  for Backing
- ½ yard (*45.7cm*) of fabric for Binding
- 3¼ yards (*297.2cm*) of Batting

CUTTING

All measurements include ¼" (0.5cm) seam allowances.

From Fabric A (navy blue), cut:
- One 12½" x 40" (*31.8cm x 101.6cm*) rectangle
- One 8½" x 37½" (*21.6cm x 95.3cm*) rectangle

From Fabric B (light blue), cut:
- One 8½" x 23½" (*21.6cm x 59.7cm*) rectangle
- One 8½" x 12½" (*21.6cm x 31.8cm*) rectangle

From Fabric C (orange), cut:
- One 12½" x 30½" (*31.8cm x 77.5cm*) rectangle
- One 8½" x 15½" (*21.6cm x 39.4cm*) rectangle
- One 8½" x 12½" (*21.6cm x 31.8cm*) rectangle

From Fabric D (pale pink), cut:
- One 15½" x 37½" (*39.4cm x 95.3cm*) rectangle
- One 15½" (*39.4cm*) square
- One 8½" x 30½" (*21.6cm x 77.5cm*) rectangle

From Fabric E (white), cut:
- One 15½" x 37½" (*39.4cm x 95.3cm*) rectangle
- One 12½" (*31.8cm*) square
- One 8½" (*21.6cm*) square

Finished Size: 50½" x 65½"
(*128.3cm x 166.4cm*)
Skill Level: Beginner
Fabrics Used: Kona Cottons
in Amber, Ballet Slipper,
Cornflower, Copen, and White

Pieced by Elizabeth Chappell
Quilted by Jill Johnson of J Coterie

PIECING

1. Sew RST one Fabric A 12½" x 40" (*31.8cm x 101.6cm*) rectangle and one Fabric E 12½" (*31.8cm*) square. Press seam toward Fabric A.

2. Sew RST one Fabric C 8½" x 12½" (*21.6cm x 31.8cm*) rectangle on the bottom of the Fabric E piece.

3. Draw one diagonal line from corner to corner of the wrong side of one Fabric D 15½" (*39.4cm*) square.

4. Pin RST one Fabric D 15½" (*39.4cm*) square on the top of one Fabric E 15½" x 37½" (*39.4cm x 95.3cm*) rectangle, making sure the drawn diagonal line is face up.

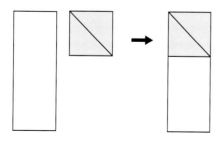

5. Sew ON the drawn line and trim ¼" (*0.5cm*) away from the sewn line. Open and press seam toward Fabric D.

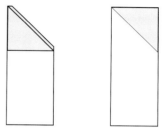

6. Sew RST one Fabric A 8½" x 37½" (*21.6cm x 95.3cm*) rectangle with the pieced rectangle from step 5. Note the placement and direction of the sewn Fabric D on Fabric E. Press seam toward Fabric A.

7. Sew RST one Fabric D 15½" x 37½" (*39.4cm x 95.3cm*) rectangle with your rectangle from step 6. Press seam toward Fabric D.

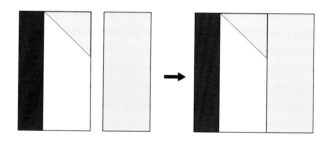

8. Sew RST one Fabric B 8½" x 23½" (*21.6cm x 59.7cm*) rectangle with one Fabric C 8½" x 15½" (*21.6cm x 39.4cm*) rectangle. Press seam in one direction.

9. Sew RST one Fabric B 8½" x 12½" (*21.6cm x 31.8cm*) rectangle with one Fabric C 12½" x 30½" (*31.8cm x 77.5cm*) rectangle. Press seam in one direction.

10. Sew RST one Fabric E 8½" (*21.6cm*) square with one Fabric D 8½" x 30½" (*21.6cm x 77.5cm*) rectangle. Press seam in one direction.

11. Sew RST one at a time your sewn strips from steps 8, 9, and 10. Press seams in one direction.

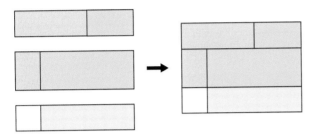

12. Sew RST units from steps 7 and 11. Press seam in one direction.

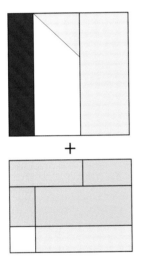

13. On the left side of the unit from step 12, sew the rectangle from step 2. Press seam in one direction. The finished quilt top measures 50½" x 65½" (*128.3cm x 166.4cm*).

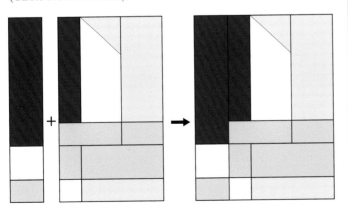

FINISHING

See Materials and Cutting sections (page 26) for materials needed for finishing. Follow Basting (page 17), Quilting (page 18), and Binding (page 19) instructions to finish your quilt.

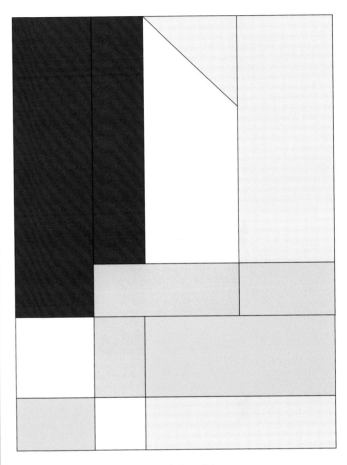

Day Trip Quilt Top Diagram

DESERT SONG

There is something visually appealing about the offset lines in this design. Notice the larger lined section in the middle with offset lines that are less wide on the sides. The design is clean, simple, yet sophisticated. It makes the perfect statement quilt for a home, and would look dashing draped on a couch or chair.

MATERIALS

Yardage is based on 42" (106.7cm)–wide fabric.

	Pillow (20" x 20" [50.8cm x 50.8cm])	Baby (35" x 52" [88.9cm x 132.1cm])	Throw (61½" x 68" [156.2cm x 172.7cm])
Fabric A (light brown)	⅜ yard (34.3cm)	1 yard (91.4cm)	¾ yard (68.6cm)
Fabric B (white)	⅜ yard (34.3cm)	1 yard (91.4cm)	1¾ yards (160cm)
Backing	1½ yards (137.2cm)	2½ yards (228.6cm)	4 yards (365.8cm)
Binding	N/A	½ yard (45.7cm) cut into five 2½" x WOF (6.4cm x WOF) strips	⅝ yard (57.2cm) cut into seven 2½" x WOF (6.4cm x WOF) strips
Batting	N/A	2½ yards (228.6cm)	4 yards (365.8cm)

CUTTING

All measurements include ¼" (0.5cm) seam allowances.

	Pillow (20½" x 20½" [52.1cm x 52.1cm])	Baby (35½" x 52½" [90.2cm x 133.4cm])	Throw (62" x 68½" [157.5cm x 174cm])
Fabric A (light brown)	Two 4½" x WOF (11.4cm x WOF) strips, then *subcut:* • Two 4½" x 12½" (11.4cm x 31.8cm) strips • Six 4½" x 4½" (11.4cm x 11.4cm) strips	Seven 4½" x WOF (11.4cm x WOF) strips, then *subcut:* • Six 4½" x 21½" (11.4cm x 54.6cm) strips • Fourteen 4½" x 7½" (11.4cm x 19.1cm) strips	Ten 4½" x WOF (11.4cm x WOF) strips, reserve seven 4½" x WOF (11.4cm X WOF) strips From four strips, *subcut:* • Sixteen 4½" x 10½" (11.4cm x 26.7cm) strips
Fabric B (white)	Two 4½" x WOF (11.4cm x WOF) strips, then *subcut:* • Three 4½" x 12½" (11.4cm x 31.8cm) strips • Four 4½" x 4½" (11.4cm x 11.4cm) strips	Six 4½" x WOF (11.4cm x WOF) strips, then *subcut:* • Seven 4½" x 21½" (11.4cm x 54.6cm) strips • Twelve 4½" x 7½" (11.4cm x 19.1cm) strips	Twelve 4½" x WOF (11.4cm x WOF) strips, reserve eight 4½" x WOF (11.4cm X WOF) strips From four strips, *subcut:* • Fourteen 4½" x 10½" (11.4cm x 26.7cm) strips

Finished Sizes: Pillow (20" x 20" [50.8cm x 50.8cm]),
Baby (35" x 52" [88.9cm x 132.1cm]), and Throw (61½" x 68" [156.2cm x 172.7cm])
Skill Level: Beginner
Fabrics Used: Art Gallery Fabrics pure solids in Mink and Crème de la Crème

Pieced by Jamie McPheeters, Quilted by Cheryl Tessitore

PIECING

The following steps use the measurements of the Baby size quilt top. You can replace the sizes and rows and columns depending on what finished size you are making. Use Piecing Table as a reference.

PIECING TABLE

	Pillow (20½" x 20½" [52.1cm x 52.1cm])	Baby (35½" x 52½" [90.2cm x 133.4cm])	Throw (62" x 68½" [157.5cm x 174cm])
Sizes of fabric you are working with	12½" x 4½" (31.8cm x 11.4cm) strips 4½" x 4½" (11.4cm x 11.4cm) strips	21½" x 4½" (54.6cm x 11.4cm) strips 7½" x 4½" (19.1cm x 11.4cm) strips	4½" x WOF (11.4cm x WOF) strips 4½" x 10½" (11.4cm x 26.7cm) strips
Rows and columns you will make	Rows - 5 Columns - 3	Rows - 13 Columns – 3	Rows - 17 Columns - 3

1. Piece RST one Fabric A 7½" x 4½" (*19.1cm x 11.4cm*) strip with one Fabric B 7½" x 4½" (*19.1cm x 11.4cm*) strip. Press seam toward the darker fabric.

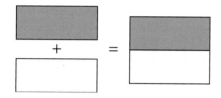

2. Continue piecing your 7½" x 4½" (*19.1cm x 11.4cm*) strips RST, alternating between Fabrics A and B until you have one completed row of thirteen strips. Repeat these steps to make one more identical row of thirteen alternating Fabrics A and B 7½" x 4½" (*19.1cm x 11.4cm*) strips. Make sure each row starts and ends with a Fabric A strip.

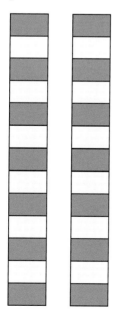

3. Piece RST one Fabric B 21½" x 4½" (*54.6cm x 11.4cm*) strip with one Fabric A 21½" x 4½" (*54.6cm x 11.4cm*) strip. Press seam toward the darker fabric.

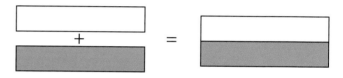

4. Continue piecing your 21½" x 4½" (*54.6cm x 11.4cm*) strips RST, alternating between Fabrics B and A until you have one completed row of thirteen strips. Make sure each row starts and ends with a Fabric B strip.

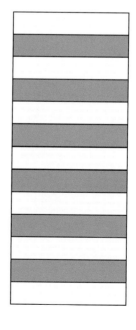

5. Pin one 7½" x 4½" (*19.1cm x 11.4cm*) row RST to the right side of your 21½" x 4½" (*54.6cm x 11.4cm*) row.

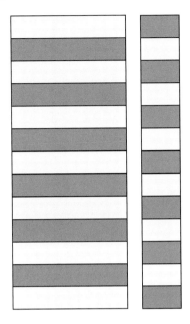

6. Sew ¼" (*0.5cm*) from the edge of the pinned rows. Press seams in one direction.

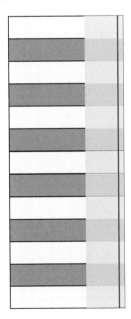

7. Pin one 7½" x 4½" (*19.1cm x 11.4cm*) row RST to the left side of your 21½" x 4½" (*54.6cm x 11.4cm*) row.

8. Sew ¼" (*0.5cm*) from the edge of the pinned rows. Press seams in one direction. To make a pillow or throw size, repeat steps 1 through 7, changing out your fabric sizes, rows, and columns using Piecing Table as a guide.

FINISHING

See Materials and Cutting sections (page 30) for materials needed for finishing. Follow Basting (page 17), Quilting (page 18), and Binding (page 19) instructions to finish your quilt. If making a pillow, follow the Making a Pillow instructions (page 22) instead.

Desert Song Quilt Top Diagram

GRAND STAIRCASE

The name for this quilt comes from a place in southern Utah with precariously balanced natural rock formations that inspired the design of this quilt. When making this design, you can refer to the tetradic color theory guide (page 12) to choose fabrics. It's fun to mix and match four harmonious colors. The finished size of this quilt makes a perfect baby quilt or can make a stunning wall display.

MATERIALS

Yardage is based on 42" (106.7cm)–wide fabric.

- ¼ yard (22.9cm) or one fat quarter in Fabric A (gray)
- ¼ yard (22.9cm) or one fat quarter in Fabric B (yellow)
- ¼ yard (22.9cm) or one fat quarter in Fabric C (red)
- ⅞ yard (80cm) in Fabric D (peach)
- ½ yard (45.7cm) of fabric for Background (white)
- 1⅝ yards (148.6cm)* of fabric for Backing
- ½ yard (45.7cm) of fabric for Binding
- 40" x 56" (101.6cm x 142.2cm) of Batting

Backing assumes at least 4" (10.2cm) overage on all sides.

CUTTING

All measurements include ¼" (0.5cm) seam allowances.

From Fabric A (gray), cut:
- One 20½" x 3½" (52.1cm x 8.9cm) rectangle
- One 15½" x 3½" (39.4cm x 8.9cm) rectangle
- One 10½" x 3½" (26.7cm x 8.9cm) rectangle
- One 5½" x 3½" (14cm x 8.9cm) rectangle

From Fabric B (yellow), cut:
- One 20½" x 3½" (52.1cm x 8.9cm) rectangle
- One 15½" x 3½" (39.4cm x 8.9cm) rectangle
- One 10½" x 3½" (26.7cm x 8.9cm) rectangle
- One 5½" x 3½" (14cm x 8.9cm) rectangle

From Fabric C (red), cut:
- One 20½" x 3½" (52.1cm x 8.9cm) rectangle
- One 15½" x 3½" (39.4cm x 8.9cm) rectangle
- One 10½" x 3½" (26.7cm x 8.9cm) rectangle
- One 5½" x 3½" (14cm x 8.9cm) rectangle

From Fabric D (peach), cut:
- Three 6½" x WOF (16.5cm x WOF) strips for side borders
- Two 3½" x WOF (8.9cm x WOF) strips, then *subcut*:
  - One 20½" x 3½" (52.1cm x 8.9cm) rectangle
  - One 15½" x 3½" (39.4cm x 8.9cm) rectangle
  - One 10½" x 3½" (26.7cm x 8.9cm) rectangle
  - One 5½" x 3½" (14cm x 8.9cm) rectangle

From Background (white), cut:
- Four 3½" x WOF (8.9cm x WOF) strips, then *subcut*:
  - Eight 8" x 3½" (20.3cm x 8.9cm) rectangles
  - Eight 5½" x 3½" (14cm x 8.9cm) rectangles
  - Eight 3" x 3½" (7.6cm x 8.9cm) rectangles

Finished Size: 32½" x 48½" (*82.6cm x 123.2cm*)
Skill Level: Beginner
Fabrics Used: Art Gallery Fabric Pure Solids in Ocean Fog, Honey,
Toasty Walnut, Terracotta, and Crème de la Crème

Pieced by Jamie McPheeters, Quilted by Cheryl Tessitore

PIECING

1. Arrange Fabric A strips and two each of the small, medium, and large Background strips as shown in the diagram. Refer to the following figure for steps 1 through 6.

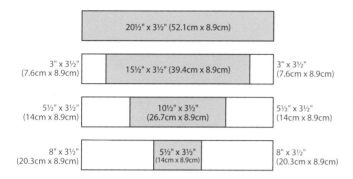

	20½" x 3½" (52.1cm x 8.9cm)
3" x 3½" (7.6cm x 8.9cm)	15½" x 3½" (39.4cm x 8.9cm) — 3" x 3½" (7.6cm x 8.9cm)
5½" x 3½" (14cm x 8.9cm)	10½" x 3½" (26.7cm x 8.9cm) — 5½" x 3½" (14cm x 8.9cm)
8" x 3½" (20.3cm x 8.9cm)	5½" x 3½" (14cm x 8.9cm) — 8" x 3½" (20.3cm x 8.9cm)

2. Sew strips together to make four rows. Press seams open. Each rows measures 20½" x 3½" (*52.1cm x 8.9cm*).

3. Sew rows together to complete the unit. Press seams open. Unit measures 20½" x 12½" (*52.1cm x 31.8cm*).

4. Repeat steps 1 through 3 to make Fabric B, Fabric C, and Fabric D units.

5. Sew Fabric A-D unit together in a single column. Press seams open. The Center column measures 20½" x 48½" (*52.1cm x 123.2cm*).

6. Sew 6½" (*16.5cm*) Fabric C strips together end-to-end. Cut two 6½" x 48½" (*16.5cm x 123.2cm*) side borders and sew to the left and right sides of the center column. Press seams toward the borders.

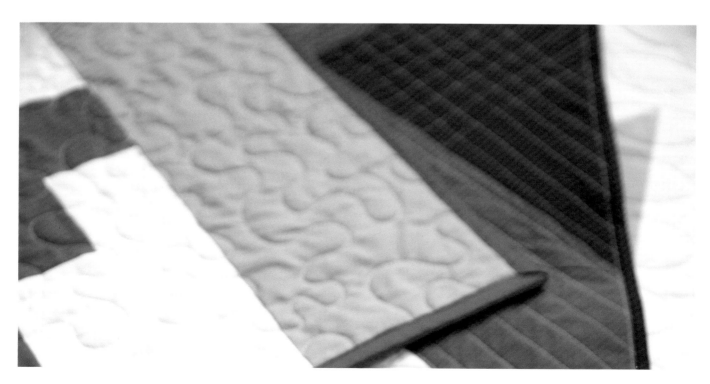

FINISHING

See Materials and Cutting sections (page 34) for materials needed for finishing. Follow Basting (page 17), Quilting (page 18), and Binding (page 19) instructions to finish your quilt.

Grand Staircase Quilt Top Diagram

RIVERWOODS

Named for one of my favorite areas in Utah, this monochromatic geometric design features two patterns in one, either as side-by-side wall hangings or made as individual pieces. I decided not to put a binding on mine and instead put them inside a picture frame. This is a fun and unique way to display your quilt as art in your home but feel free to finish yours however you like!

MATERIALS

Yardage is based on 42" (106.7cm)–wide fabric.

	One Panel	Both Panels
Fabric A (dark green)	¼ yard (22.9cm) or one fat quarter	¼ yard (22.9cm) or one fat quarter
Fabric B (light green)	¼ yard (22.9cm) or one fat quarter	¼ yard (22.9cm) or one fat quarter
Fabric C (yellow green)	One 10" (25.4cm) square	Two 10" (25.4cm) squares
Background (white)	½ yard (45.7cm)	1 yard (91.4cm)
Backing	¾ yard (68.6cm)	1½ yards (137.2cm)
Binding	¼ yard (22.9cm)	½ yard (45.7cm)
Batting	One 24" x 30" (61cm x 76.2cm) piece	Two 24" x 30" (61cm x 76.2cm) pieces

CUTTING

All measurements include ¼" (0.5cm) seam allowances. Fabric A-C instructions below are for only Panel 1 or Panel 2. If making both panels, cut two of each piece.

- From Fabric A (dark green), cut one 14½" x 7½" (36.8cm x 19.1cm) rectangle, fold in half to make a 7¼" x 7½" (18.4cm x 19.1cm) rectangle and *subcut* one Template A semicircle
- From Fabric B (light green), cut one 14½" x 7½" (36.8cm x 19.1cm) rectangle, fold in half to make a 7¼" x 7½" (18.4cm x 19.1cm) rectangle and *subcut* one Template A semicircle
- From Fabric C (yellow green), cut one 7½" (19.1cm) square, then *subcut* one Template C quarter circle

For Panel 1, from Background (white), cut:
- Two 14½" x 9½" (36.8cm x 24.1cm) rectangles, fold each in half to make 7¼" x 9½" (18.4cm x 24.1cm) rectangles, then *subcut* two Template B
- One 9½" x 7½" (24.1cm x 19.1cm) rectangle

- One 7½" (19.1cm) square, then *subcut* one Template D
- One 18½" x 2½" (47cm x 6.4cm) strip
- One 18½" x 1½" (47cm x 3.8cm) strip

For Panel 2, from Background (white), cut:
- Two 14½" x 9½" (36.8cm x 24.1cm) rectangle, fold each in half to make 7¼" x 9½" (18.4cm x 24.1cm) rectangles, then *subcut* two Template B
- One 7½" (19.1cm) square, then *subcut* one Template D
- One 9½" x 6½" (24.1cm x 16.5cm) rectangle
- One 18½" x 2½" (47cm x 6.4cm) strip
- One 9½" x 2½" (24.1cm x 6.4cm) strip
- One 7½" x 2½" (19.1cm x 6.4cm) strip
- One 9½" x 1½" (24.1cm x 3.8cm) strip

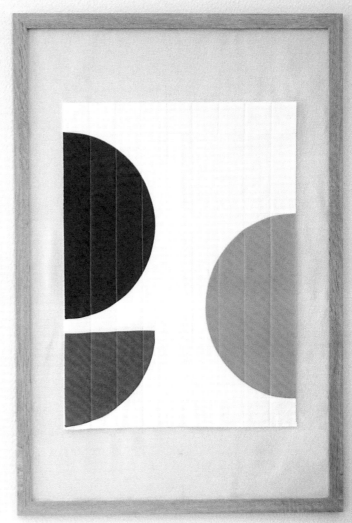

Finished Size: 18½" x 24½" (*47cm x 62.2cm*)
Skill Level: Advanced Beginner
Fabrics Used: Art Gallery Fabrics Snow, Eucalyptus, Fresh Sage, and Kona Cottons in Laurel

....

Pieced and quilted by Jamie McPheeters

PIECING

QUARTER CIRCLES

Make one Fabric C unit for one panel or two units to make both panels.

1. Gather Template C (Fabric C) and Template D (Background) pieces. Starting with one concave and one convex piece, fold each in half and finger press to make a crease at the center of each curve.

2. Place the concave piece on top of the convex piece, RST. Align centers and pin.

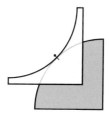

3. Align each end of the concave piece flush with the edges of the convex piece and pin.

4. Pin along the rest of the curve as desired, then sew a ¼" (0.5cm) seam along the curve.

5. Press seam open or toward the darker fabric. The unit measures 7½" (19.1cm) square.

SEMICIRCLES

Make one Fabric A and one Fabric B unit for either panel or two units of each to make both panels.

1. Gather Template A (Fabric A) and Template B (Background) pieces. Starting with one concave and one convex piece, fold each in half and finger press to make a crease at the center of each curve. Fold each side in half again and make a crease at the quarter and three-quarters points along each curve.

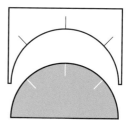

2. As with the quarter circles, place the concave piece on the convex piece, RST. Align centers and pin.

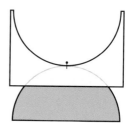

3. Align each end of the concave piece flush with the edges of the convex piece and pin.

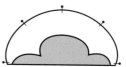

4. Pin the quarter and three-quarters points, and along the rest of the curve as desired, then sew a ¼" (0.5cm) seam.

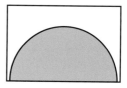

5. Repeat steps 1 through 4 to make a second semicircle unit from Fabric B. Each unit measures 14½" x 7½" (36.8cm x 19.1cm).

ASSEMBLY

For quilt top assembly, refer to the panel assembly diagrams below. Use the arrows shown in the diagrams as indication of which direction to press your seams.

PANEL 1

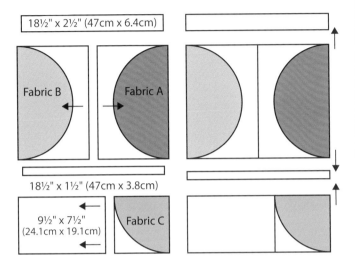

18½" x 2½" (47cm x 6.4cm)

18½" x 1½" (47cm x 3.8cm)

9½" x 7½" (24.1cm x 19.1cm)

Fabric B

Fabric A

Fabric C

PANEL 2

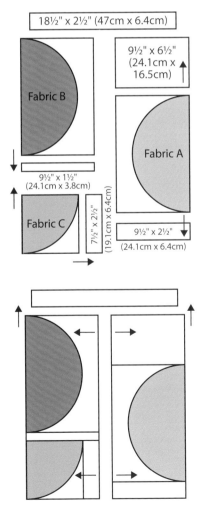

18½" x 2½" (47cm x 6.4cm)

9½" x 6½" (24.1cm x 16.5cm)

Fabric B

Fabric A

9½" x 1½" (24.1cm x 3.8cm)

Fabric C

7½" x 2½" (19.1cm x 6.4cm)

9½" x 2½" (24.1cm x 6.4cm)

FINISHING

See Materials and Cutting sections for materials needed for finishing. Follow Basting (page 17) instructions and Quilt (page 18) as you desire. I decided not to bind my quilt top to give it a more natural look. But if you want to bind your panels, cut three 2½" x WOF (6.4cm x WOF) strips (for one panel) or six 2½" x WOF (6.4cm x WOF) strips (for two panels) from the binding fabric. Stitch together end to end with diagonal seams. Finish using the Binding (page 19) instructions.

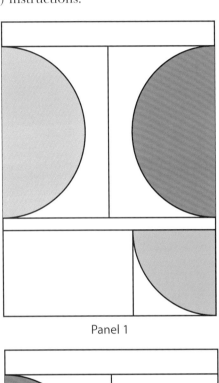

Panel 1

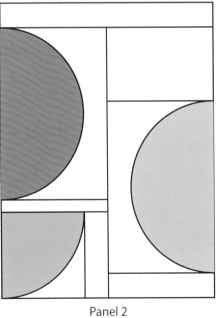

Panel 2

Riverwoods Quilt Top Diagrams

RIVERWOODS TEMPLATES

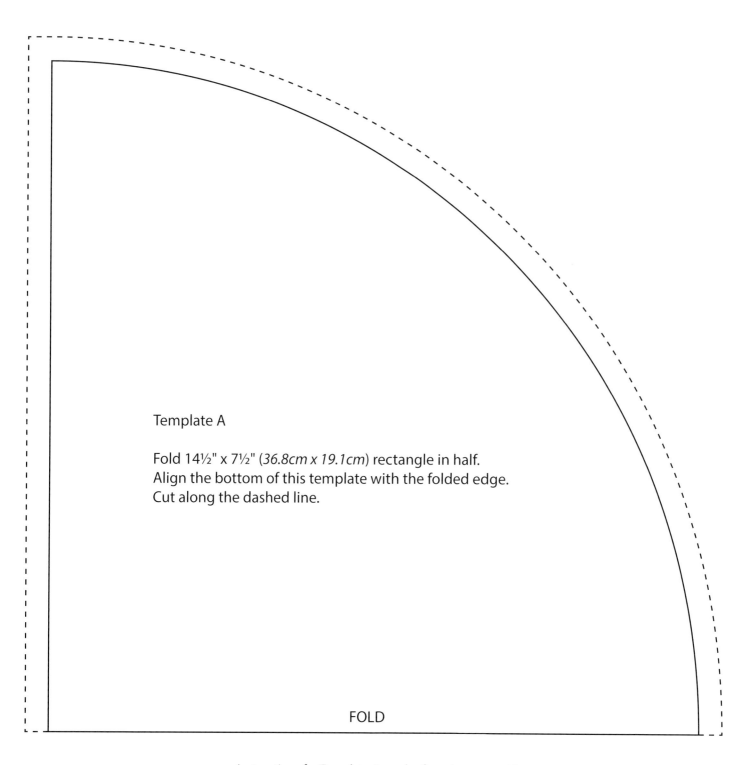

Template A

Fold 14½" x 7½" (*36.8cm x 19.1cm*) rectangle in half.
Align the bottom of this template with the folded edge.
Cut along the dashed line.

FOLD

Instructions for Template A can be found on page 40.

FOLD

Template B

Fold 14½" x 9½" (*36.8cm x 24.1cm*) rectangle in half.
Align the right edge of this template with the folded edge.
Cut along the dashed line.

Instructions for Template B can be found on page 40.

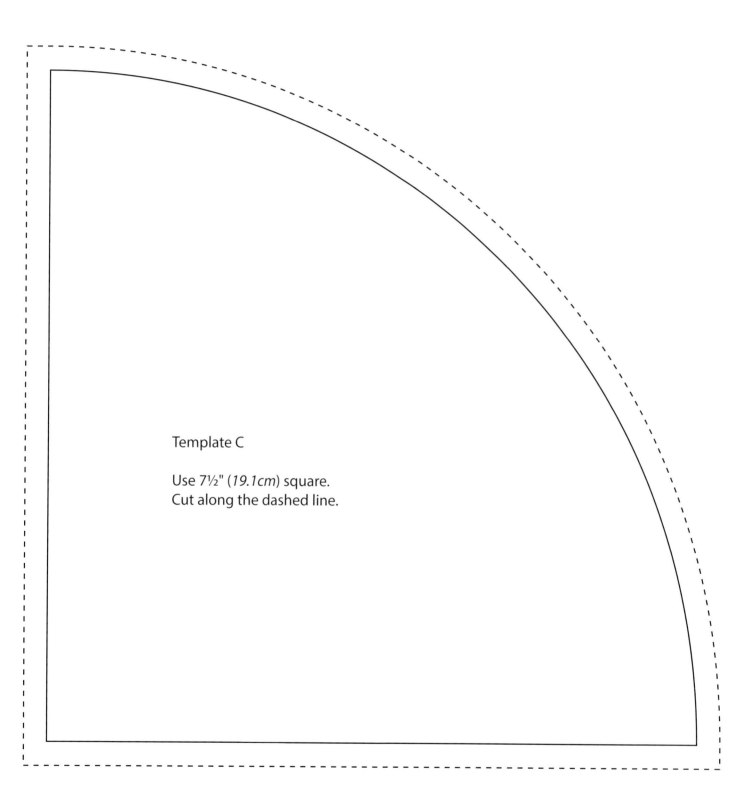

Template C

Use 7½" (*19.1cm*) square.
Cut along the dashed line.

Instructions for Template C can be found on page 40.

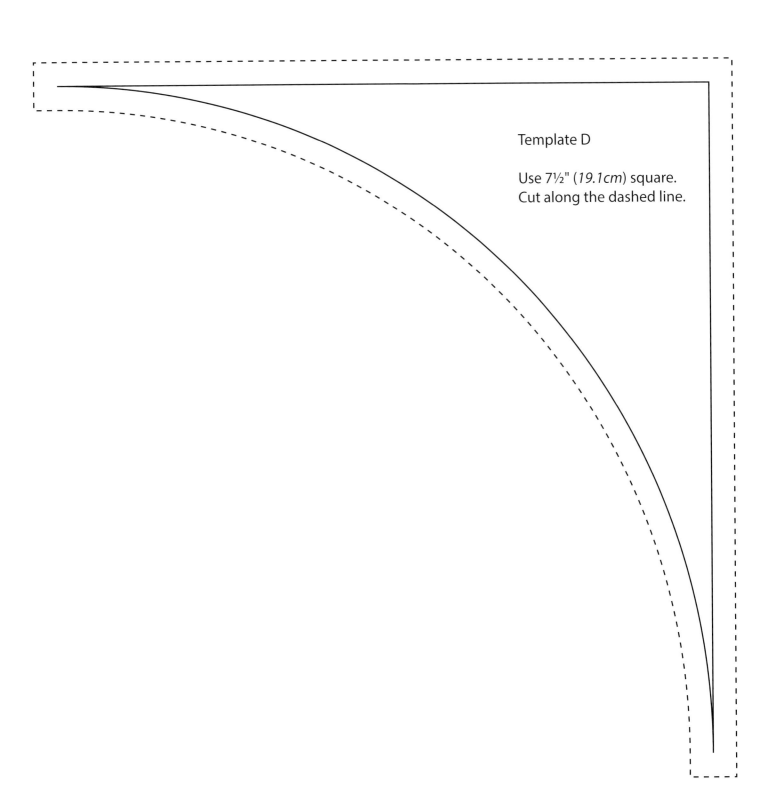

Template D

Use 7½" (*19.1cm*) square.
Cut along the dashed line.

Instructions for Template D can be found on page 40.

MORNING HIKE

The only difficult thing about this pattern is finding enough fabrics in one color with different shades and tones to achieve the ombre look. It was intentional to have two lighter fabrics on the left and then go drastically darker, then slowly lighter again as the eye moves to the right of the quilt. I used a mixture of orange fabrics from my stash, with the background being Art Gallery Fabrics pure solids in Snow.

MATERIALS

Yardage is based on 42" (106.7cm)–wide fabric.

- Eleven ⅜ yard (34.3cm) cuts, one each in Fabrics A-K (darker ombre fabrics)
- Six ¼ yard (22.9cm) cuts, one each in Fabrics L-Q (lighter ombre fabrics)
- 2⅜ yards (217.2cm) in of fabric for Background (white)
- ¾ yard (68.6cm) of fabric for Binding
- 5½ yards (475.5cm) of fabric for Backing
- 5½ yards (475.5cm) of Batting

CUTTING

All measurements include ¼" (0.5cm) seam allowances.

From Background (white), cut:
- Seventeen 4½" x WOF (11.4cm x WOF) strips, trim selvage edges and sew strips together along the short edges to make one long, continuous strip. *Subcut the following strips from the continuous strip:*
  - Row 1: One 4½" x 30½" (11.4cm x 77.5cm) strip
  - Row 2: One 4½" x 21½" (11.4cm x 54.6cm) strip
  - Row 3: One 4½" x 16½" (11.4cm x 41.9cm) strip
  - Row 4: One 4½" x 9½" (11.4cm x 24.1cm) strip
  - Row 5: One 4½" x 12½" (11.4cm x 31.8cm) strip
  - Row 6: One 4½" x 15½" (11.4cm x 39.4cm) strip
  - Row 7: One 4½" x 23½" (11.4cm x 59.7cm) strip
  - Row 8: One 4½" x 26½" (11.4cm x 67.3cm) strip
  - Row 9: One 4½" x 32½" (11.4cm x 82.6cm) strip
  - Row 10: One 4½" x 38½" (11.4cm x 97.8cm) strip
  - Row 11: One 4½" x 41½" (11.4cm x 105.4cm) strip
  - Row 12: One 4½" x 52½" (11.4cm x 133.4cm) strip
  - Row 13. One 4½" x 58½" (11.4cm x 148.6cm) strip
  - Row 14: One 4½" x 61½" (11.4cm x 156.2cm) strip
  - Row 15: One 4½" x 67½" (11.4cm x 171.5cm) strip
  - Row 16: One 4½" x 76½" (11.4cm x 194.3cm) strip
  - Row 17: One 4½" x 80½" (11.4cm x 204.5cm) strip

From Fabrics A-Q, first decide order of your fabric colors, referring to diagram in Piecing section (page 49).
Cut your strips as follows:
- Row 1: Two 4½" x WOF (11.4cm x WOF) strips, trim to one 4½" x 60½" (11.4cm x 153.7cm) strip
- Row 2: Two 4½" x WOF (11.4cm x WOF) strips, trim to one 4½"x 69½" (11.4cm x 176.5cm) strip
- Row 3: Two 4½" x WOF (11.4cm x WOF) strips, trim to one 4½" x 74½" (11.4cm x 189.2cm) strip
- Row 4: Two 4½" x WOF (11.4cm x WOF) strips, trim to one 4½" x 81½" (11.4cm x 207cm) strip

Cutting continued on next page

Finished Size:
68½" x 90½" (*174cm x 229.9cm*)
Skill Level: Beginner
Fabrics Used: Colored strips are a variety of fabrics from stash, background fabric is Snow from Art Gallery Fabrics

Pieced by Elizabeth Chappell
Quilted by Jill Johnson of J Coterie

- Row 5: Two 4½" x WOF (*11.4cm x WOF*) strips, trim to one 4½" x 78½" (*11.4cm x 199.4cm*) strip
- Row 6: Two 4½" x WOF (*11.4cm x WOF*) strips, trim to one 4½" x 75½" (*11.4cm x 191.8cm*) strip
- Row 7: Two 4½" x WOF (*11.4cm x WOF*) strips, trim to one 4½" x 67½" (*11.4cm x 171.5cm*) strip
- Row 8: Two 4½" x WOF (*11.4cm x WOF*) strips, trim to one 4½" x 64½" (*11.4cm x 163.8cm*) strip
- Row 9: Two 4½" x WOF (*11.4cm x WOF*) strips, trim to one 4½" x 58½" (*11.4cm x 148.6cm*) strip
- Row 10: Two 4½" x WOF (*11.4cm x WOF*) strips, trim to one 4½" x 52½" (*11.4cm x 133.4cm*) strip
- Row 11: Two 4½" x WOF (*11.4cm x WOF*) strips, trim to one 4½" x 49½" (*11.4cm x 125.7cm*) strip
- Row 12: One 4½" x WOF (*11.4cm x WOF*) strip, trim to one 4½" x 38½" (*11.4cm x 97.8cm*) strip
- Row 13: One 4½" x WOF (*11.4cm x WOF*) strip, trim to one 4½" x 32½" (*11.4cm x 82.6cm*) strip
- Row 14: One 4½" x WOF (*11.4cm x WOF*) strip, trim to one 4½" x 29½" (*11.4cm x 74.9cm*) strip
- Row 15: One 4½" x WOF (*11.4cm x WOF*) strip, trim to one 4½" x 23½" (*11.4cm x 59.7cm*) strip
- Row 16: One 4½" x WOF (*11.4cm x WOF*) strip, trim to one 4½" x 14½" (*11.4cm x 36.8cm*) strip
- Row 17: One 4½" x WOF (*11.4cm x WOF*) strip, trim to one 4½" x 10½" (*11.4cm x 26.7cm*) strip

From Binding cut:
- Nine 2½" x WOF (*6.4cm x WOF*) strips

From Backing cut:
- Two 99" x WOF (*251.5cm x WOF*) strips, remove selvages and sew strips together along the trimmed edges to create one 99" x 83" (*251.5cm x 210.8cm*) rectangle, trim to 77" x 99" (*195.6cm x 251.5cm*) rectangle

NOTES

- If you want the gradient effect of the quilt shown, I suggest going to a fabric store in-person or choosing your fabric from fabric swatches to make sure the fabrics you choose go well together and give the desired look.

- Keep a pencil handy. Draw a line through each strip as you work through the pattern. It makes remembering which strip you are working on easier. When you are done, you can erase your lines.

PIECING

1. Referring to diagram below, sew Fabrics A and B for Row 1 RST. Press seam open. Row 1 should measure 4½" x 90½" (*11.4cm x 229.9cm*).

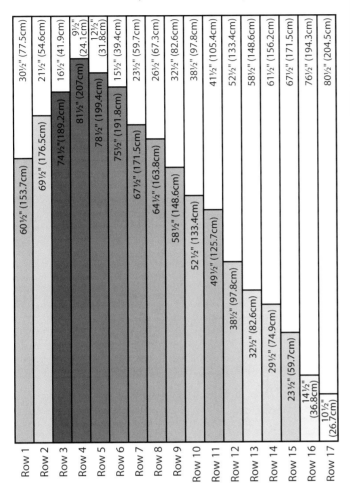

30½" (77.5cm)	21½" (54.6cm)	16½" (41.9cm)	9½" (24.1cm)	12½" (31.8cm)	15½" (39.4cm)	23½" (59.7cm)	26½" (67.3cm)	32½" (82.6cm)	38½" (97.8cm)	41½" (105.4cm)	52½" (133.4cm)	58½" (148.6cm)	61½" (156.2cm)	67½" (171.5cm)	76½" (194.3cm)	80½" (204.5cm)
60½" (153.7cm)	69½" (176.5cm)	74½" (189.2cm)	81½" (207cm)	78½" (199.4cm)	75½" (191.8cm)	67½" (171.5cm)	64½" (163.8cm)	58½" (148.6cm)	52½" (133.4cm)	49½" (125.7cm)	38½" (97.8cm)	32½" (82.6cm)	29½" (74.9cm)	23½" (59.7cm)	14½" (36.8cm)	10½" (26.7cm)
Row 1	Row 2	Row 3	Row 4	Row 5	Row 6	Row 7	Row 8	Row 9	Row 10	Row 11	Row 12	Row 13	Row 14	Row 15	Row 16	Row 17

2. Continue sewing Rows 2-17 RST, pressing seams open. Each row should measure 4½" x 90½" (*11.4cm x 229.9cm*) when finished. Press seams open.

ASSEMBLY

1. Starting with Row 1, sew Rows 1 and 2, RST. Press seam to one side.

2. Continuing in order, sew Rows 2–17, RST. Press seams to one side. Continue until the entire quilt top is pieced together. Finished quilt top measures 68½" x 90½" (*174cm x 229.9cm*).

FINISHING

See Materials and Cutting sections (pages 46 and 48) for materials needed for finishing. Follow Basting (page 17), Quilting (page 18), and Binding (page 19) instructions to finish your quilt.

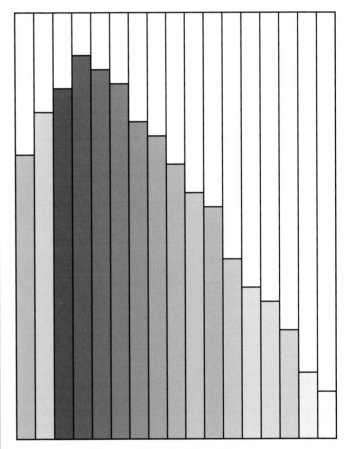

Morning Hike Quilt Top Diagram

Using a fun, color-coordinating printed fabric as a backing makes for the perfect finishing touch!

MOUNTAIN PEAK

The angled strips in this design remind me of the peaks of a mountain, hence the name. This design is great for playing with patterned fabrics and bold color palettes in a color block quilt, like in the quilt shown. However, you could also use gradient fabrics, a monochromatic palette, or even a two-color striped pattern instead to match your home's décor better.

MATERIALS

Yardage is based on 42" (106.7cm)–wide fabric.

- ¼ yard (22.9cm) each of Fabrics A-I (warm and neutral-toned colors)
- 2⅜ yards (217.2cm) of fabric for Backing
- ½ yard (45.7cm) of fabric for Binding
- 2⅜ yards (217.2cm) of Batting

CUTTING

All measurements include ¼" (0.5cm) seam allowances.

From Fabrics A - I, fold all strips in half, matching short ends to crease in the center, and cut a total of:
- Two 2" x WOF (5cm x WOF) strips. Select a fabric you want to run down the middle of your quilt, and piece into one long continuous 2" (5cm) strip
- Four 2¾" (7cm) squares. For a scrappier look, use different fabrics for each of your squares
- Four 2" x 7" (5cm x 17.8cm) strips
- Four 2" x 10½" (5cm x 26.7cm) strips
- Four 2" x 13" (5cm x 33cm) strips
- Four 2" x 17" (5cm x 43.2cm) strips
- Four 2" x 20" (5cm x 50.8cm) strips
- Four 2" x 22" (5cm x 55.9cm) strips
- Thirty 2" x 25" (5cm x 63.5cm) strips

From Binding, cut:
- Five 2½" x WOF (6.4cm x WOF) strips

NOTES

- To get the scrappy look like the quilt shown, cut your fabrics in random order.
- I recommend starching your fabric before cutting.
- Using a good quilter's cotton helps get your pieces accurate. While lovely, I found that more loosely woven fabrics, like the ones used in the quilt shown, made the strips a bit tricky. When a fabric is more loosely woven, it tends to stretch easily. When fabrics stretch while quilting, it can make your piecing not be accurate. So for any quilt, the more dense the thread count (or tighter the threads are woven together), the more accurate your piecing will be. But especially with this pattern where you are cutting your strips at an angle, I recommend using quilting cotton.

Finished Size:
34" x 44" (*86.4cm x 111.8cm*)
Skill Level: Intermediate
Fabric Used: Warp and Weft by
Ruby Star Society

Pieced by Jamie McPheeters
Quilted by Cheryl Tessitore

PIECING

1. Cut one 2¾" (*7cm*) square in half, from corner to corner. Fold your triangle piece in half and finger press so there is a crease down the middle. Note: you do not need to use the other half of your square for this pattern.

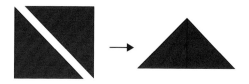

2. Place one 2" x 7" (*5cm x 17.8cm*) strip RST with your triangle from the previous step. Align the folded center creases and pin them in place. Ensure there is a 1½" (*3.8cm*) overhang on both sides of the triangle piece. Sew using a ¼" (*0.5cm*) seam along the 4" (*10.2cm*) side of the triangle shown with the dotted line.

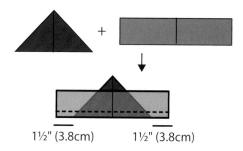

1½" (3.8cm)   1½" (3.8cm)

3. Press seam in one direction. It's really important to PRESS the seam and not iron it (aka don't move your iron around) as the movement can warp your fabric.

4. Continue adding one strip at a time in the following order. Make sure to match center folded creases as you go. Press seams in one direction. Stop after you add the 2" x 25" (*5cm x 63.5cm*) strip.

- 2" x 10½" (*5cm x 26.7cm*) strip
- 2" x 13" (*5cm x 33cm*) strip
- 2" x 17" (*5cm x 43.2cm*) strip
- 2" x 20" (*5cm x 50.8cm*) strip
- 2" x 22" (*5cm x 55.9cm*) strip
- 2" x 25" (*5cm x 63.5cm*) strip

5. When you have sewn on your 2" x 25" (*5cm x 63.5cm*) strip, bring your piece to your cutting mat. Place the pieced triangle in the corner of your cutting mat.

6. With your pieced triangle in the corner of your cutting mat, use a ruler and rotary cutter to trim just the edges of your sewn rectangle pieces. Use the lines on your cutting mat and the original triangle piece from step 1 as a guide to create a triangle piece that measures 17½" x 17½" x 24¾" (*44.5cm x 44.5cm x 62.9cm*). Repeat steps 1 through 6 to make four total triangle pieces.

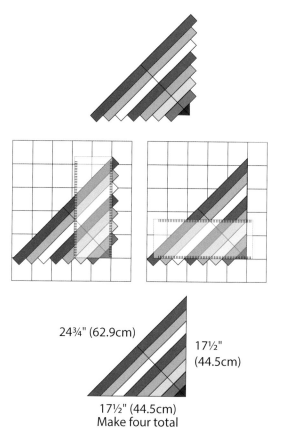

24¾" (62.9cm)   17½" (44.5cm)

17½" (44.5cm)
Make four total

TRIANGLE PIECES CUT LEFT AND RIGHT

1. Bring one triangle piece to your cutting mat. Using a ruler with a 45-degree line, place the 45-degree line on your last sewn seam. Trim along the outside edge of your ruler on the LEFT SIDE of your triangle piece. Do this for two of your triangle pieces.

Make two total
Cut from left

2. With your remaining two triangle pieces, trim in the same way but on the RIGHT SIDE of the triangle.

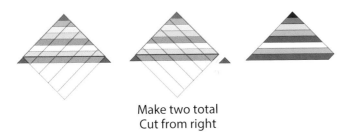

Make two total
Cut from right

MIDDLE SECTIONS

1. Sew one 2" x 25" (*5cm x 63.5cm*) strip RST with one 2" x 25" (*5cm x 63.5cm*) strip. Offset the strips by 1½" (*3.8cm*), moving the bottom strip 1½" (*3.8cm*) to the right of the top. Press seam in one direction.

1½"

2. Continue sewing strips RST one at a time, offsetting by 1½" (*3.8cm*) inches to the right. Sew a total of thirteen strips together.

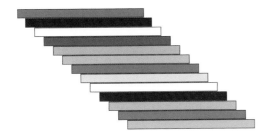

3. Repeat these steps with your remaining thirteen strip pieces; this time, offset your strips moving to the LEFT of the top strip.

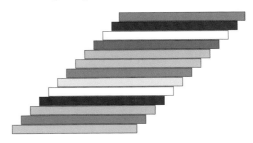

4. Bring one middle strip at a time to your cutting mat and align one of the shorter sides with a straight line on your cutting mat. Using your ruler, trim the edges of your strips. Align the ruler with the corners of your pieces and trim off just the end triangle pieces. Repeat this with both thirteen-strip pieces.

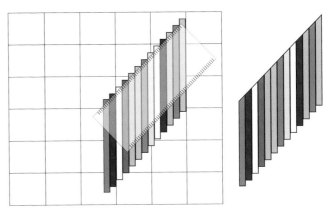

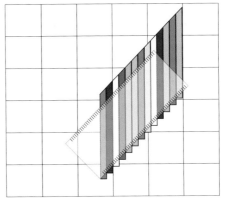

ATTACHING TRIANGLE PIECES TO MIDDLE

1. Sew RST one left trimmed triangle to one middle piece. Follow the diagram for direction on how to place the two pieces RST. There will be a ¼" (*0.5cm*) overhang of fabric on each side, shown with circles below. Press seam in one direction.

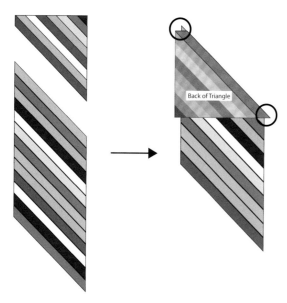

2. Sew RST one left trimmed triangle to the unit from step 1. It will have a ¼" (*0.5cm*) overhang when piecing. Press seams in same dirrection as step 1.

3. Repeat steps 1 and 2 using the right trimmed triangles and the second middle piece to make another half of your quilt top.

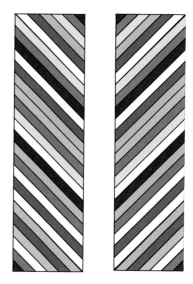

4. Sew RST one 2" x 47" (*5cm x 119.4cm*) strip to the center of one-half of your quilt top. Press seam in one direction.

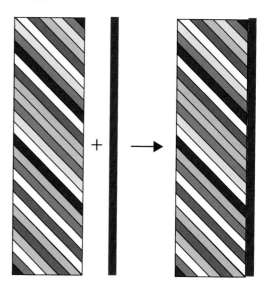

5. Sew RST the other half of your quilt top to your unit from step 3. You now have completed the quilt top.

FINISHING

See Materials and Cuttings sections (page 52) for materials needed for finishing. Follow Basting (page 17), Quilting (page 18), and Binding (page 19) instructions to finish your quilt.

Mountain Peak Quilt Top Diagram

MIRROR LAKE

This wall-art-size project can bring the look and feel of the sun setting on water indoors with the mirror effect the two semi-circles broken up with one strip of fabric in the middle creates. Mirror Lake is a great pattern to use the complementary color theory (page 12) by choosing two colors of fabric that complement each other from the color wheel for the half-circle pieces.

MATERIALS

Yardage is based on 42" (106.7cm)–wide fabric.

- One fat eighth in Fabric A (dark pink)
- One fat eighth in Fabric B (light pink)
- One fat eighth in Fabric C (yellow)
- ½ yard (45.7cm) of fabric for Background (white)
- ¾ yard* (68.6cm) of fabric for Backing
- ¼ yard (22.9cm) for fabric for Binding
- 23" x 30" (58.4cm x 76.2cm) of Batting

*Backing assumes at least 4" (10.2cm) overage on all sides.

CUTTING

All measurements include ¼" (0.5cm) seam allowances.

From Fabric A (dark pink), cut:
- One 6½" x WOF (16.5cm x WOF) strip, then *subcut:*
  - Two convex Template A (page 62) pieces

From Fabric B (light pink), cut:
- One 6½" x WOF (16.5cm x WOF) strip, then *subcut:*
  - Two convex Template A (page 62) pieces

From Fabric C (yellow), cut:
- One 17½" x 2½" (44.5cm x 6.4cm) rectangle

From Background (white), cut:
- One 4½" x WOF (11.4cm x WOF) strip, then *subcut:*
  - Two 17½" x 4½" (44.5cm x 11.4cm) rectangles
- One 8" x WOF (20.3cm x WOF) strip, then *subcut:*
  - Four concave Template B (page 63) pieces
  - Four 1½" x 7" (3.8cm x 17.8cm) rectangles

From Binding, cut:
- Three 2½" x WOF (6.4cm x WOF) strips

Finished Size:
17½" x 23½" (*44.5cm x 59.7cm*)
Skill Level: Advanced Beginner
Fabric Used: Art Gallery Fabrics in Snow,
Cotton Candy, Blossomed, and Honeydew

Pieced by Jamie McPheeters
Quilted by Cheryl Tessitore

PIECING

1. Gather Template A (Fabrics A and B) and Template B (Background) pieces using templates on pages 62 and 63. Starting with one concave and one convex piece, fold each in half and finger press to make a crease at the center of each curve.

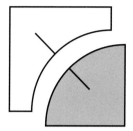

2. Place the concave piece on top of the convex piece, RST. Align centers and pin.

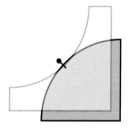

3. Align each end of the concave piece flush with the edges of the convex piece and pin.

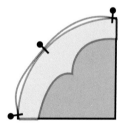

4. Pin along the rest of the curve as desired, then sew a ¼" (0.5cm) seam along the curve. Sewn line is shown by red dotted line. Press seam toward Fabric A of B.

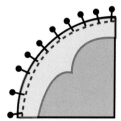

5. Repeat steps 1 through 4 to make three additional quarter circle units with the remaining Template A and Template B pieces. Each unit measures 8" (20.3cm) square.

6. Arrange the four quarter-circle blocks as shown, with Fabric A on top and Fabric B on the bottom. Each block should be rotated so that when viewed together, the four quadrants form a full circle.

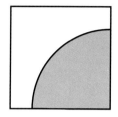

7. Trim 1" (2.5cm) from the bottom of the Fabric A block and from the top of the Fabric B blocks.

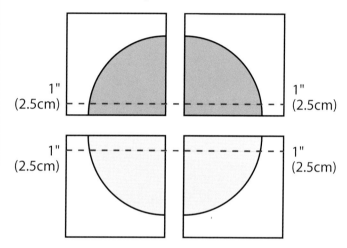

8. Pay close attention to which side of the block needs to be trimmed! Discard the resulting 1" (2.5cm) strips (indicated by the Xs in the diagram); these are not needed. The blocks now measure 8" x 7" (20.3cm x 17.8cm).

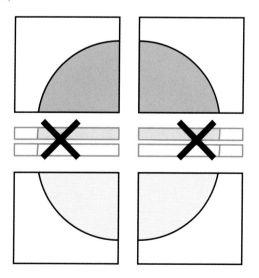

ASSEMBLY

1. Assemble the quilt top in 5 rows as shown. Press seams open.

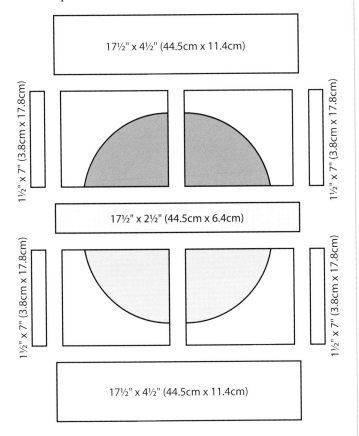

17½" x 4½" (44.5cm x 11.4cm)

1½" x 7" (3.8cm x 17.8cm)

1½" x 7" (3.8cm x 17.8cm)

17½" x 2½" (44.5cm x 6.4cm)

1½" x 7" (3.8cm x 17.8cm)

1½" x 7" (3.8cm x 17.8cm)

17½" x 4½" (44.5cm x 11.4cm)

2. Sew rows together. Press seams open.

FINISHING

See Materials and Cutting sections (page 58) for materials needed for finishing. Follow Basting (page 17), Quilting (page 18), and Binding (page 19) instructions to finish your quilt.

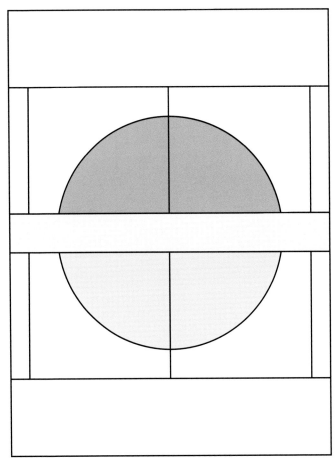

Mirror Lake Quilt Top Diagram

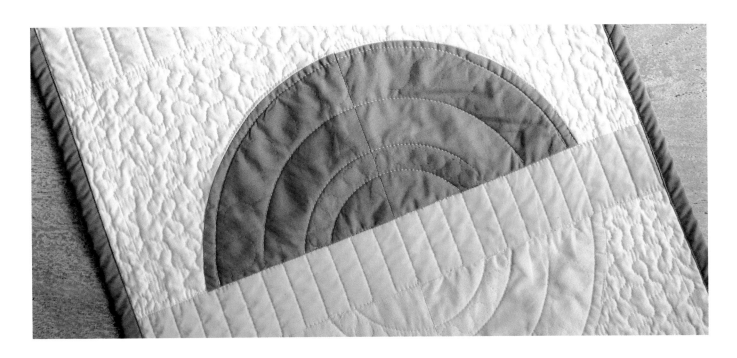

MIRROR LAKE TEMPLATES

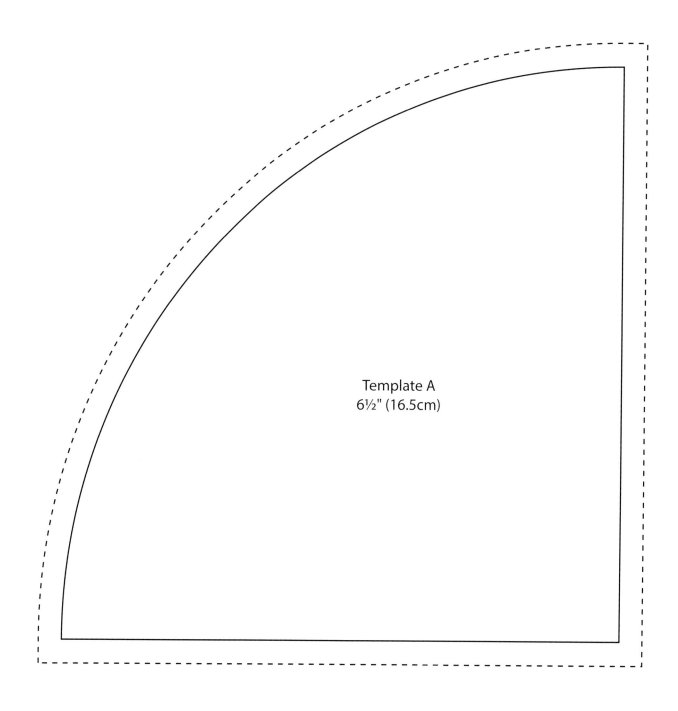

Template A
6½" (16.5cm)

Instructions for Template A can be found on page 60.

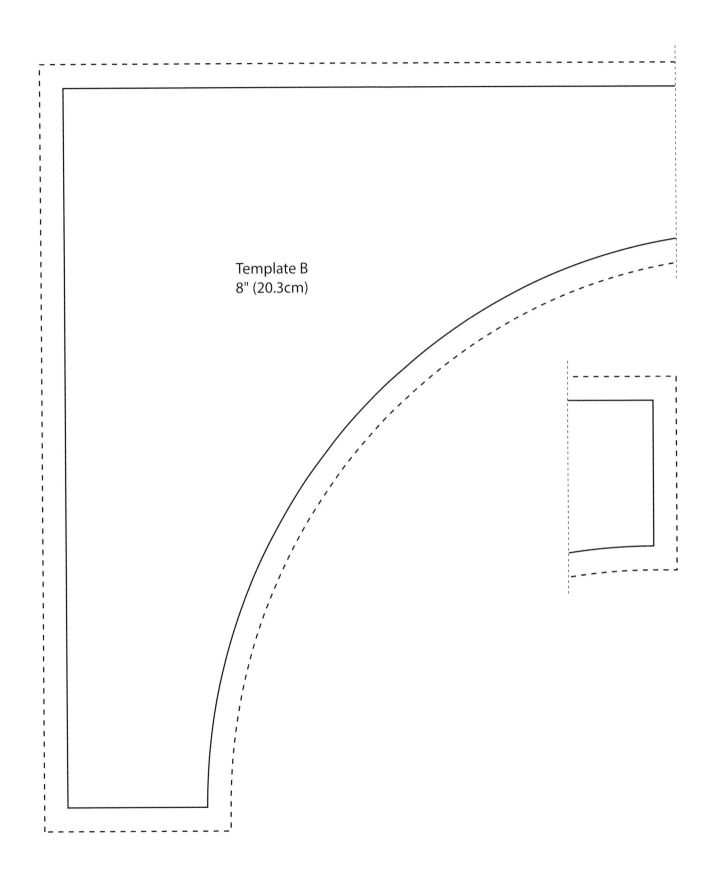

Template B
8" (20.3cm)

Instructions for Template B can be found on page 60.

SUNDANCE

Sundance is possibly my favorite place to visit, and this design, inspired by the mountainous location, also features some of my favorite colors. The quilt's modern geometric pattern works well with gradient or ombre fabrics and is also a great project to play with some fun quilting to finish your quilt. For example, the quilt shown features a simple yet stunning crisscrossing pattern created by stitching parallel to the triangle forms. I hope you enjoy the Sundance quilt pattern and maybe even the real Sundance one day if you're lucky.

MATERIALS

Yardage is based on 42" (106.7cm)–wide fabric.

	Baby (32" x 40" [81.3cm x 101.6cm])	Throw (60" x 80" [152.4cm x 203.2cm])
Fabric A (white)	¾ yard (68.6cm)	2¼ yards (205.7cm)
Fabric B (pale pink)	⅜ yard (34.3cm)	1¼ yards (114.3cm)
Fabric C (light pink)	⅜ yard (34.3cm)	1¼ yards (114.3cm)
Fabric D (medium pink)	⅜ yard (34.3cm)	1¼ yards (114.3cm)
Fabric E (rust)	⅜ yard (34.3cm)	1¼ yards (114.3cm)
Fabric F (deep red)	¼ yard (22.9cm) or one fat quarter	¼ yard (22.9cm) or one fat quarter
Backing	1⅜ yard (125.7cm)	5 yards (457.2cm)
Binding	⅜ yard (34.3cm)	⅝ yard (57.2cm)
Batting	1⅜ yard (125.7cm)	5 yards (457.2cm)

CUTTING

All measurements include ¼" (0.5cm) seam allowances.

	Baby (32" x 40" [81.3cm x 101.6cm])	Throw (60" x 80" [152.4cm x 203.2cm])
Fabric A (white)	Five 9" (22.9cm) squares / Two 8½" (21.6cm) squares	Five 17" (43.2cm) squares / Two 16½" (41.9cm) squares
Fabric B (pale pink)	Three 9" (22.9cm) squares	Three 17" (43.2cm) squares
Fabric C (light pink)	Three 9" (22.9cm) squares	Three 17" (43.2cm) squares
Fabric D (medium pink)	Three 9" (22.9cm) squares	Three 17" (43.2cm) squares
Fabric E (rust)	Three 9" (22.9cm) squares	Three 17" (43.2cm) squares
Fabric F (deep red)	One 9" (22.9cm) square	One 17" (43.2cm) square
Backing	1⅜ yards x WOF (125.7cm x WOF)	5 yards x WOF (457.2cm x WOF)
Binding	Four 2½" x WOF (6.4cm x WOF) strips	Eight 2½" x WOF (6.4cm x WOF) strips

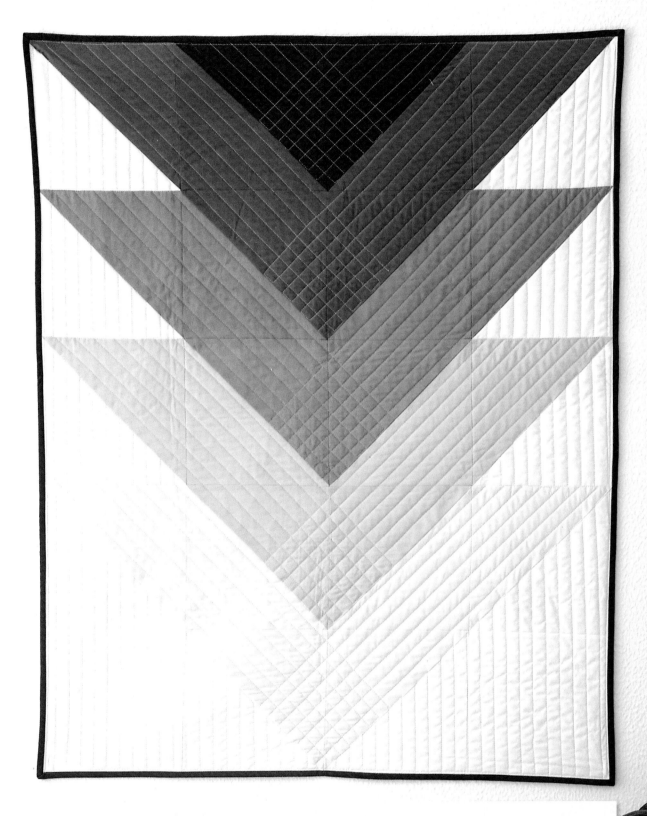

Finished Sizes: Baby (32" x 40" [*81.3cm x 101.6cm*]), and
Throw (60" x 80" [*152.4cm x 203.2cm*])
Skill Level: Advanced Beginner
Fabrics Used: Art Gallery Fabrics in White Linen, Sweet Macademia, Blushing,
Cinnamon, Terracotta, and Robert Kaufman in Cinnamon.

....

Pieced by Jamie McPheeters, Quilted by Cheryl Tesitore

PIECING

PIECING TABLE

	Fabric B	Fabric C	Fabric D	Fabric E	Fabric F
Fabric A	4	2	2	2	—
Fabric B	—	2	—	—	—
Fabric C	—	—	2	—	—
Fabric D	—	—	—	2	—
Fabric E	—	—	—	—	2

BABY SIZE QUILT

Half Square Triangles (HSTs) 8½" (*21.6cm*)

The following directions use 9" (*22.9cm*) squares and yield two 8½" (*21.6cm*) HSTs. Use the Piecing Table to see how many of each fabric combination of HSTs are needed. In the following directions, I use Fabrics A and B as an example. Switch Fabrics A and B to make your needed number of HSTs in the fabrics shown in the table.

1. Place RST one Fabric A 9" (*22.9cm*) square with one Fabric B 9" (*22.9cm*) square. Draw one diagonal line from corner to corner on the wrong side of the lighter fabric.

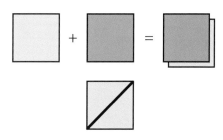

2. Sew ¼" (*0.5cm*) away from the drawn line, then cut ON the drawn line.

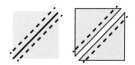

3. Press seams to one side. Trim each HST to measure 8½" (*21.6cm*) square.

4. Repeat these steps to make your total needed number of HSTs. Refer to Piecing Table.

THROW SIZE QUILT

Half Square Triangles (HSTs) 16½" (*41.9cm*)

The following directions yield two 16½" (*41.9cm*) HSTs. Use the Piecing Table to see how many of each fabric combination of HSTs are needed. In the following directions, I use Fabrics A and B as an example. Switch Fabrics A and B to make your needed number of HSTs in the fabrics shown in the table.

1. Place RST one Fabric A 17" (*43.2cm*) square with one Fabric B 17" (*43.2cm*) square. Draw one diagonal line from corner to corner on the wrong side of the lighter fabric.

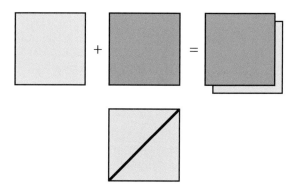

2. Sew ¼" (*0.5cm*) away from the drawn line, then cut ON the drawn line.

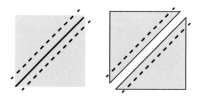

3. Press seams to one side. Trim each HST to measure 16½" (*41.9cm*) square.

4. Repeat these steps to make your total needed number of HSTs. Refer to the Piecing Table.

ASSEMBLY

1. Arrange your fabric pieces in rows and columns following the Quilt Top Diagram. Sew each row together one square at a time, RST. Press seams open.

2. Sew each row together to make the completed quilt top. Press seams open.

FINISHING

See Materials and Cutting sections (page 64) for materials needed for finishing. Follow Basting (page 17), Quilting (page 18), and Binding (page 19) instructions to finish your quilt.

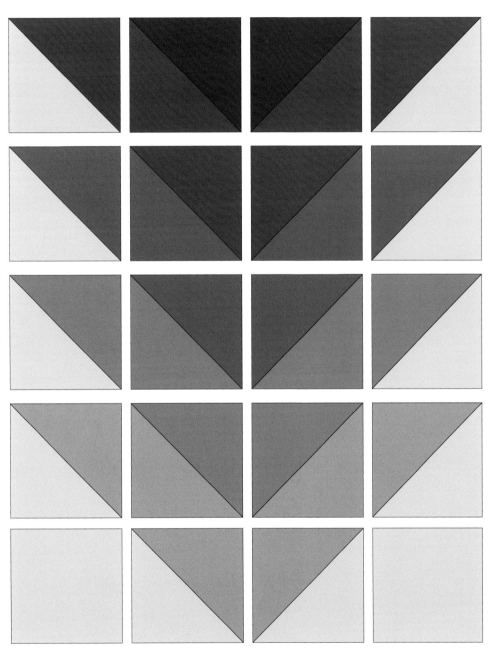

Sundance Quilt Top Diagram

HONEY

This simple hexie design was one of the first patterns I created for this book. I had no idea at the time that I would have a theme of naming so many of the projects after Utah landmarks, but since Utah is the beehive state, this was a perfect fit, and it's the perfect size for a baby quilt or to use as wall art. I love that the design is modern and makes a beautiful statement piece. It also allows for some creative and artistic quilting.

MATERIALS

Yardage is based on 42" (106.7cm)–wide fabric.

- 2 yards (*182.9cm*) in Fabric A for Background (pale blue)
- ¼ yard (*22.9cm*) or one fat quarter in Fabric B for Hexie (white)
- 1¾ yards (*160cm*)* of fabric for Backing
- ⅜ yard (*34.3cm*) of fabric for Binding
- 1. yards (*160cm*) of Batting

*Backing assumes at least 4" (10.2cm) overage on all sides.

CUTTING

All measurements include ¼" (0.5cm) seam allowances.

From Fabric A (pale blue), cut:
- Two 36½" x 12½" (*92.7cm x 31.8cm*) rectangles for top and bottom pieces
- Two 6" x 28½" (*15.2cm x 72.4cm*) side pieces
- One 21½" x 13" (*54.6cm x 33cm*) middle rectangle
- Four 15" x 8" (*38.1cm x 20.3cm*) rectangles for hexie piecing

From Fabric B (white), cut:
- Two 2½" x 13" (*6.4cm x 33cm*) rectangles for the sides
- Four 16½" x 3" (*41.9cm x 7.6cm*) hexie strips

From Binding fabric, cut:
- Five 2½" x WOF (*6.4cm x WOF*) strips

NOTES

- Standard copy paper works well for paper piecing.
- Lower the stitch length on your sewing machine. This will make the paper easy to tear away when the block is finished. I like to use a stitch length of around 1½" (*3.8cm*).
- Start sewing three to four stitches ahead of the sewing line and keep going three to four stitches past the end of the sewing line. Backstitch at the beginning and end so paper removal is easy and secure.
- Cutting and sewing through paper will dull your needle and rotary blade. Plan to change your needle and blade when you finish.

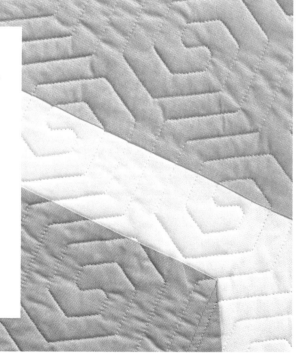

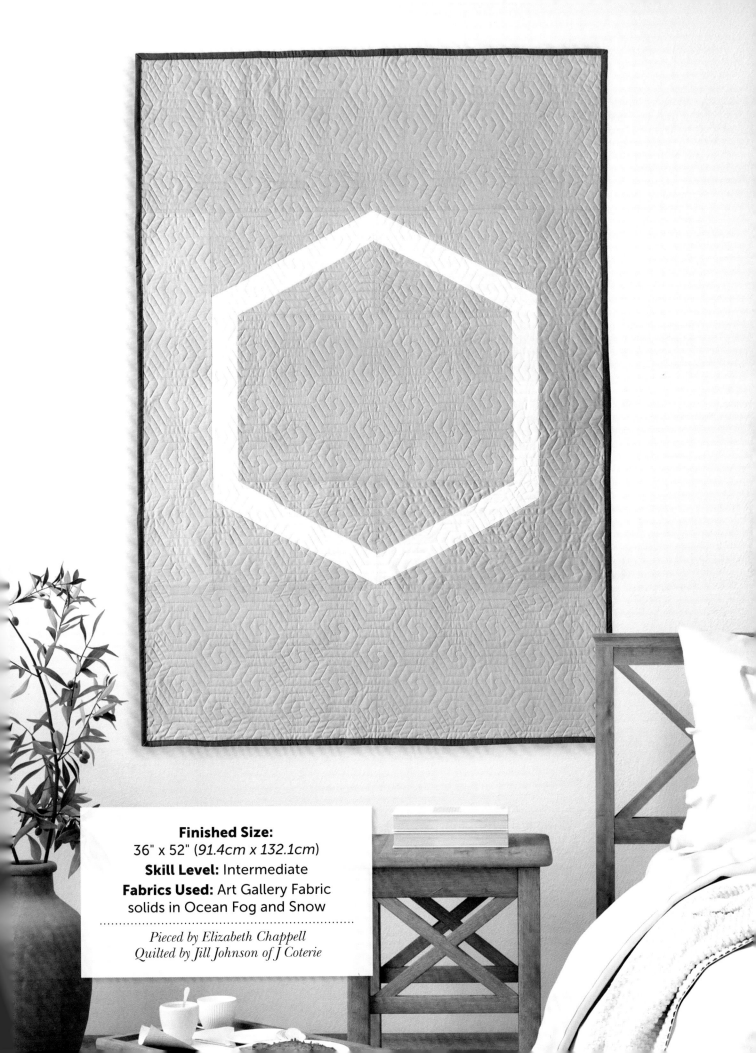

Finished Size:
36" x 52" (*91.4cm x 132.1cm*)

Skill Level: Intermediate

Fabrics Used: Art Gallery Fabric solids in Ocean Fog and Snow

Pieced by Elizabeth Chappell
Quilted by Jill Johnson of J Coterie

PIECING

1. Photocopy templates A1 and A2 from pages 74 and 77. Tape the templates together so the triangles align. Do the same with templates B1 and B2 from pages 75 and 76.

2. Cut four Fabric A 15" x 8" (*38.1cm x 20.3cm*) rectangles from corner to corner, two as shown below on top, and two as shown in below bottom. Make sure fabric is right side up when cutting.

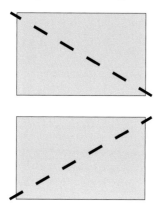

3. With your template face down, place one Fabric A triangle over the A1 template piece. Make sure the fabric is on the non-printed side of your paper. Your fabric will be right side up and should completely cover the A1 section with at least ¼" (*0.5cm*) overhang on all sides. Use a pin to keep the fabric in place.

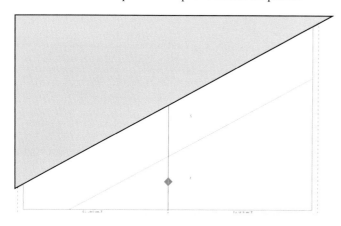

4. Place one Fabric B 16½" x 3" (*41.9cm x 7.6cm*) strip on top of your Fabric A triangle, RST. Match the edges as shown by the dotted line. Pin to your template.

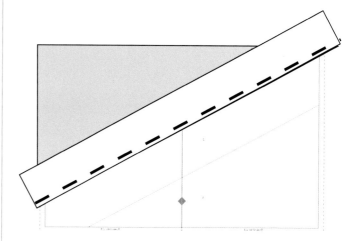

5. With Fabrics A and B pinned in place, flip your template over so the marked side is facing up. Bring template and fabrics to your sewing machine, sew ON the line between 1 and 2, shown by red dotted line. Sew a few stitches before and after the line. Be sure you make your stitch length shorter for this.

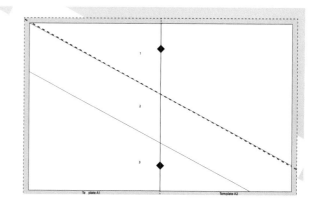

6. With your paper template still on top, fold your template back along your sewn line. See dotted line. Trim your fabric seams to be ¼" (*0.5cm*) away from your template's folded line.

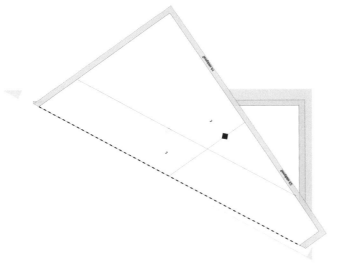

7. Open template flat and flip over so the fabric is on top. Use an iron to press the seams.

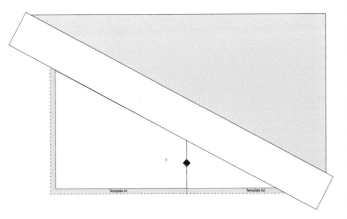

8. Match the long edge (shown by dotted line) of one Fabric A triangle with the edge of Fabric B, RST. Pin in place.

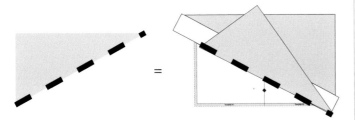

9. Bring template and fabrics to your sewing machine, sew ON the line between 2 and 3, shown by red dotted line. Sew a few stitches before and after the line. Be sure you make your stitch length shorter for this.

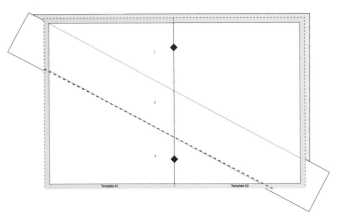

10. Flip the paper over so the fabric is on top. Use an iron to press the seams. Trim your block ON the outer dotted line of the template. Remove paper. Press seams to one side. Block measures 13" x 8¼" (*33cm x 21cm*).

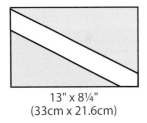

13" x 8¼"
(33cm x 21.6cm)

11. Repeat steps to make two Blocks with templates A1 and A2 and two Blocks with templates B1 and B2. Gently tear away paper templates.

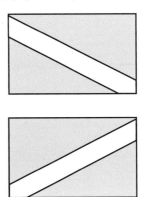

ASSEMBLY

1. Sew two Paper Piece blocks RST, one from templates A1 and A2, the other from templates B1 and B2. Make sure the blocks align as shown below. Make one Half Hexie Block measuring 25½" x 8¼" (*64.8cm x 21cm*). Press seams open.

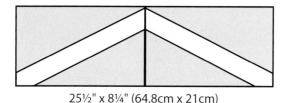

25½" x 8¼" (64.8cm x 21cm)

2. Repeat step 1 to make two 25½" x 8¼" (*64.8cm x 21cm*) blocks.

3. Sew two Fabric B 2½" x 13" (*6.4cm x 33cm*) strips RST on opposite sides of one Fabric A 21½" x 13" (*54.6cm x 33cm*) rectangle. Make sure the Fabric B strips are on the short sides of the rectangle. Press seams open. Make one Hexie Middle that measures 25½" x 13" (*64.8cm x 33cm*).

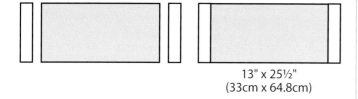

13" x 25½"
(33cm x 64.8cm)

4. Sew two Half Hexie Blocks RST on the top and bottom of one Hexie Middle Block. Press seams to one side. Hexie Block measures 25½" x 28½" (*64.8cm x 72.4cm*).

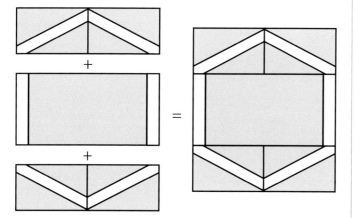

5. Sew two Fabric A 6" x 28½" (*15.2cm x 72.4cm*) strips, RST, on opposite sides of your Hexie Block. Press seams in one direction. Block should measure 36½" x 28½" (*92.7cm x 72.4cm*).

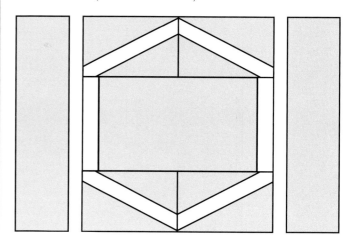

6. Sew two Fabric A 36½" x 12½" (*92.7cm x 31.8cm*) strips, RST, on top and bottom of your Hexie Block. Press seams in one direction. The finished quilt top should measure 36½" x 52½" (*92.7cm x 133.4cm*).

FINISHING

See Materials and Cutting sections (page 68) for materials needed for finishing. Follow Basting (page 17), Quilting (page 18), and Binding (page 19) instructions to finish your quilt.

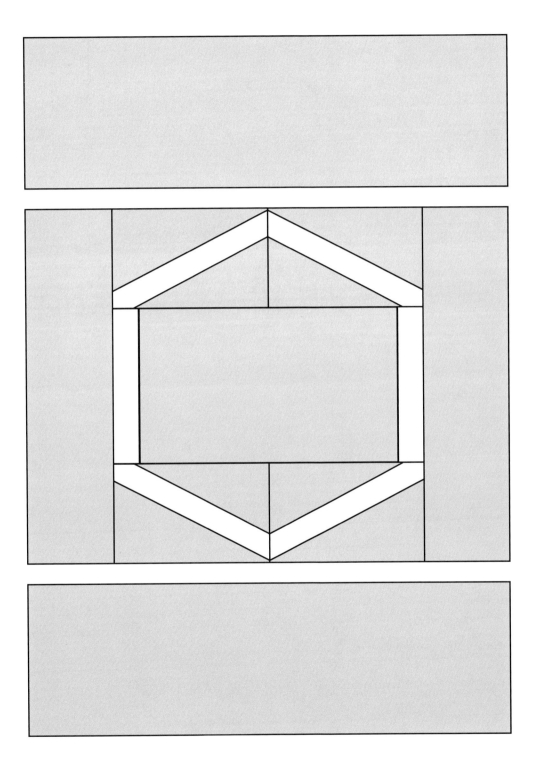

Honey Quilt Top Diagram

HONEY TEMPLATES

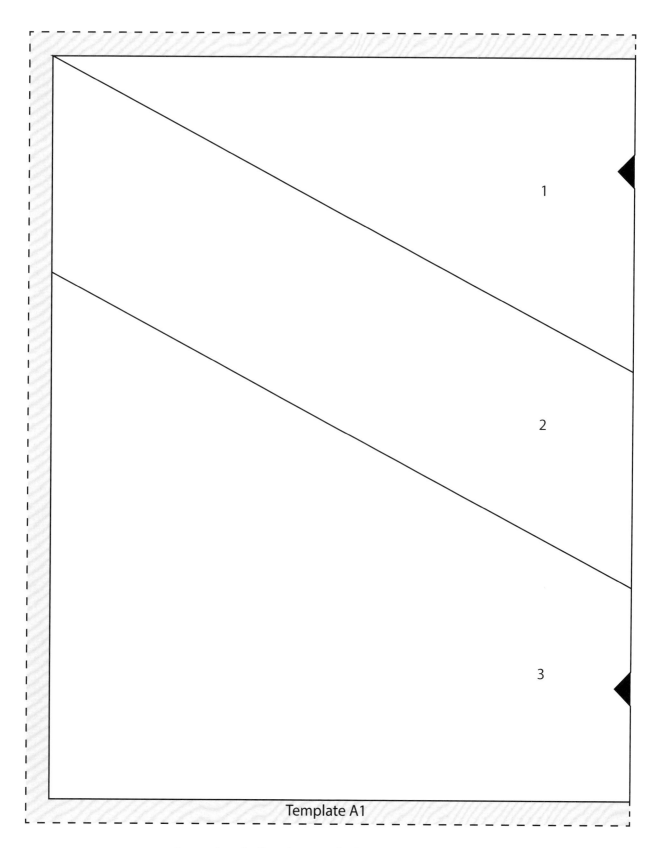

Template A1

Instructions for Templates can be found on pages 70–72.

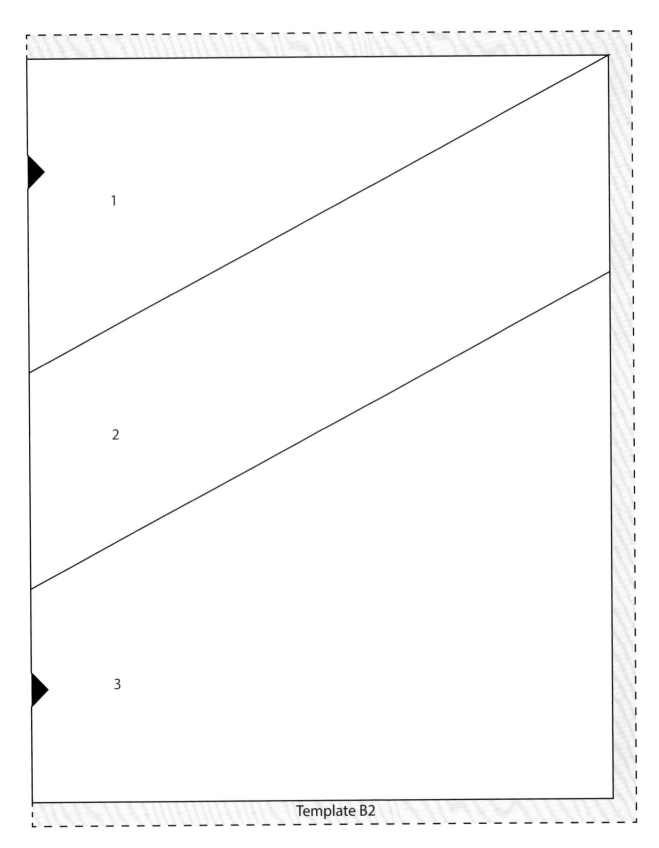

Template B2

Instructions for Templates can be found on pages 70–72.

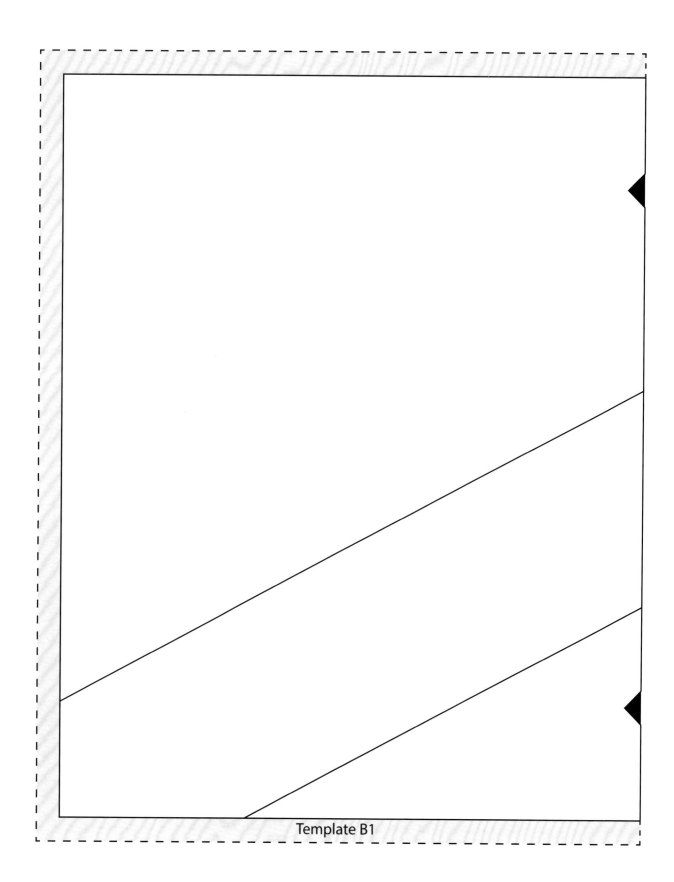

Template B1

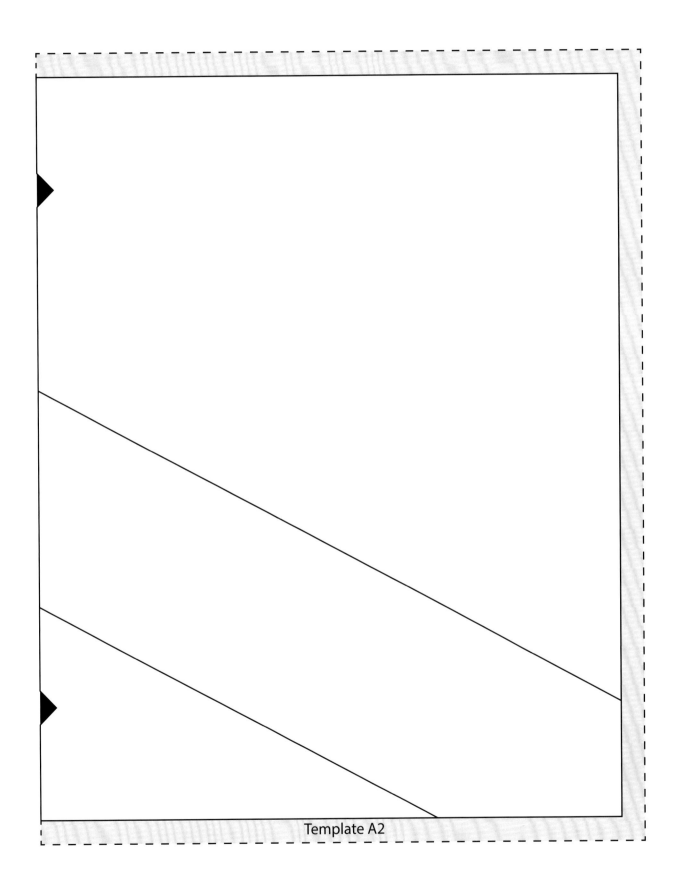

Template A2

NARROWS

I love making decorative pillows and have more in my home and on my bed than I like to admit since they are typically a lot quicker and easier to work up. The Narrows pillow is an excellent newbie-quilter project, as you can experiment and quilt the pillow cover any way you'd like. It's small enough to do some fun quilting you might not want to spend the time doing on a larger project, so have fun with it! I made my Narrows pillow with just two colors, but you could play around with the design and add multiple colors.

MATERIALS

Yardage is based on 42" (106.7cm)–wide fabric.

- ½ yard (45.7cm) in Fabric A (white) Background
- ½ yard (45.7cm) in Fabric B (blue)
- ½ yard (45.7cm) of fabric for Pillow Backing

CUTTING

All measurements include ¼" (0.5cm) seam allowances.

From Fabric A (white), cut:
- One 2½" x 10" (6.4cm x 25.4cm) strip
- One 2½" x 24½" (6.4cm x 62.2cm) strip
- One 4½" x 20" (11.4cm x 50.8cm) strip
- One 13½" x 16" (34.3cm x 40.6cm) rectangle

From Fabric B (blue), cut:
- One 2½" x 18" (6.4cm x 45.7cm) strip
- One 4½" x 10" (11.4cm x 25.4cm) strip
- One 13½" x 23" (34.3cm x 58.4cm) strip

From Pillow Backing, cut:
- Two 2" x 14" (5cm x 35.6cm) rectangles

When making a pillow, you get to quilt the pillow cover any way you'd like. Pillows are small enough that you can do some fun quilting you might not want to spend the time doing on a larger project. Have fun with it!

Finished Size:
20" x 20" (*50.8cm x 50.8cm*)
Skill Level: Advanced Beginner
Fabric Used: Golden Hour by
Ruby Star Society and Crème de la
Crème by Art Gallery Fabrics.

Pieced and quilted by
Elizabeth Chappell

PIEICING

TOP ROW

1. Place RST one Fabric A 4½" x 20" (*11.4cm x 50.8cm*) strip with one Fabric B 4½" x 10" (*11.4cm x 25.4cm*). Make sure the strips are placed as shown. There should be a ½" (*1.5cm*) overhang of fabric shown by arrows. Pin in place.

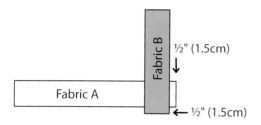

2. Draw one diagonal line as shown in red. Sew ON the red line. Trim ¼" (*0.5cm*) away from your sewn line. Trim dog ears. Press seam open. Strip should measure 4½" x 24½" (*11.4cm x 62.2cm*).

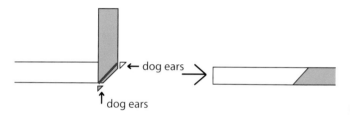

MIDDLE ROW

1. Place RST one Fabric B 2½" x 18" (*6.4cm x 45.7cm*) strip with one Fabric A 2½" x 10" (*6.4cm x 25.4cm*) strip. Make sure the strips are placed as shown. There should be a ½" (*1.5cm*) overhang of fabric shown by arrows. Pin in place.

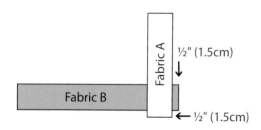

2. Draw one diagonal line as shown in red. Sew ON the red line. Trim ¼" (*0.5cm*) away from your sewn line. Trim dog ears. Press seam open. Strip should measure 2½" x 24½" (*6.4cm x 62.2cm*).

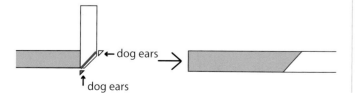

BOTTOM ROW

1. Place RST one Fabric A 13½" x 16" (*34.3cm x 40.6cm*) strip with one Fabric B 13½" x 23" (*34.3cm x 58.4cm*) strip. Make sure the strips are placed as shown. There should be a ½" (*1.5cm*) overhang of fabric shown by arrows. Pin in place.

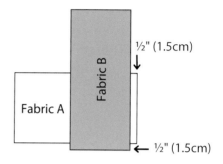

2. Draw one diagonal line as shown in red. Sew ON the red line. Trim ¼" (*0.5cm*) away from your sewn line. Trim dog ears. Press seams open. Strip should measure 13½" x 24½" (*34.3cm x 62.2cm*).

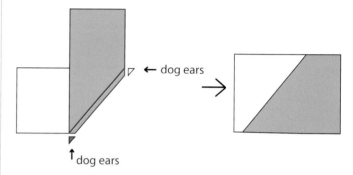

ASSEMBLY

Taking one Fabric A 2½" x 24½" (*6.4cm x 62.2cm*) strip and the Top, Middle, and Bottom rows, sew each row RST, one at a time, as shown in Pillow Top Diagram. Press seams to one side. Trim top to measure 21" x 21" (*53.3cm x 53.3cm*).

FINISHING

See Materials and Cutting sections (page 78) for materials needed for finishing. Follow Making a Pillow instructions (page 22) to finish.

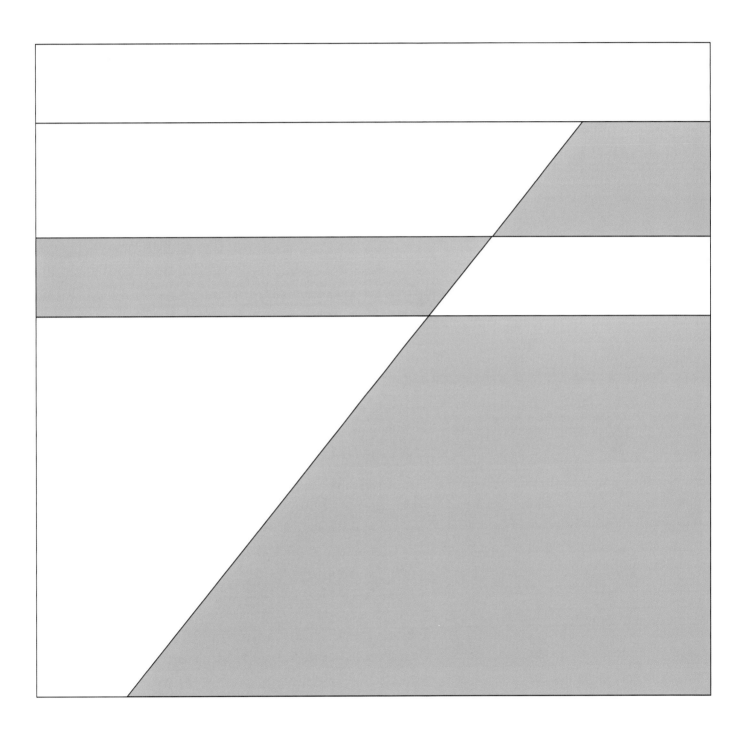

Narrows Pillow Top Diagram

TRAVEL POSTS

Since getting out and exploring the world brings inspiration both to my quilting and to my life, I wanted this quilt to be a reminder to you to venture out and experience new things as well. Inspired by hiking posts that tell you how close you are to your destination, this design works up pretty easily, making for an ideal beginner-friendly quilt or the perfect project for experienced quilters to experiment with and make their own. Try playing with colors, patterned fabrics, unique quilting, or if you're feeling extra daring, hand-embroidered destination names on the sign pieces (just make sure to do this before finishing to hide your threads in your quilt sandwich).

MATERIALS

Yardage is based on 42" (106.7cm)–wide fabric.

- ¼ yard (22.9cm) each of seven Colored Fabrics (orange, blue, red, yellow, green, beige, and teal)
- 2 yards (182.9cm) in Background (white)
- 3 yards* (274.3cm) of fabric for Backing
- ½ yard (45.7cm) of fabric for Binding
- 53" x 68" (134.6cm x 172.7cm) of Batting

*Backing assumes at least 4" (10.2cm) overage on all sides.

CUTTING

All measurements include ¼" (0.5cm) seam allowances.

Select two Colored Fabrics for the longer posts (shown as orange and blue); the remaining five Colored Fabrics will be used for the shorter posts (red, yellow, green, beige, and teal), from the first two fabrics, cut:
- One 26½" x 5" (67.3cm x 12.7cm) rectangle
- Two 2¾" (7cm) squares

From the remaining five fabrics, cut:
- One 20½" x 5" (52.1cm x 12.7cm) rectangle
- Two 2¾" (7cm) squares

From Background (white), cut:
- Five 5" x WOF (12.7cm x WOF) strips, then *subcut:*
  - Five 23¼" x 5" (59.1cm x 12.7cm) rectangles
  - Two 17¼" x 5" (43.8cm x 12.7cm) rectangles
  - Seven 2¾" x 5" (7cm x 12.7cm) rectangles
  - Three 4¼" x WOF (10.8cm x WOF) strips for top/bottom borders
  - Seven 4" x WOF (10.2cm x WOF) strips for sashing

From Binding, cut:
- Six 2½" x WOF (6.4cm x WOF) strips

From Backing, cut:
- Two 54" x WOF (137.2cm x WOF) strips, trim selvages and sew together along the long sides to make a 54" x 80" (137.2cm x 203.2cm) backing, and trim to 54" x 68" (137.2cm x 172.7cm)

Finished Size: 45½" x 60½" (*115.6cm x 153.7cm*)
Skill Level: Beginner
Fabric Used: Art Gallery Fabrics Pure Solids in Ocean Fog, Warm Wave, Sandstone, Dried Moss, Honey, Terracotta, Dried Roses, and Snow

Pieced by Jamie McPheeters, Quilted by Cheryl Tessitore

PIECING

FLYING GEESE

Make seven Flying Geese units, one for each of the seven Colored Fabrics. Each unit measures 2¾" x 5" (*7cm x 12.7cm*).

1. Draw a diagonal line from corner to corner on the wrong side of all 2¾" (*7cm*) squares.

2. Align one 2¾" (*7cm*) square with the left side of one 2¾" x 5" (*7cm x 12.7cm*) Background rectangle as shown. Sew along the marked line.

3. Trim seam allowance to ¼" (*0.5cm*), discarding the excess.

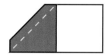

4. Open the unit and press the seam away from the center.

5. Align the remaining matching 2¾" (*7cm*) square with the right side of the rectangle and repeat steps 2 through 4 to finish the flying geese unit.

6. Repeat steps 2 through 5 with remaining colored squares and 2¾" x 5" (*7cm x 12.7cm*) Background rectangles. Make seven total flying geese units.

ASSEMBLY

Each row is made of one Colored Fabric rectangle, a matching flying geese unit, and one Background fabric rectangle.

1. Sew rows RST, one piece at a time, using the Quilt Top Diagram as a guide. Press seams open. Each row measures 45½" x 5" (*115.6cm x 12.7cm*).

- Short posts (Rows 1, 3, 4, 5, and 6) use a 20½" x 5" (*52.1cm x 12.7cm*) Colored Fabric rectangle, a flying geese unit, and a 23¼" x 5" (*59.1cm x 12.7cm*) Background rectangle.

- Long posts (Rows 2 and 7) use a 26½" x 5" (*67.3cm x 12.7cm*) Colored Fabric rectangle, a flying geese unit, and a 17¼" x 5" (*43.8cm x 12.7cm*) Background rectangle.

2. Sew 4" x WOF (*10.2cm x WOF*) strips together end to end. Cut six 4" x 45½" (*10.2cm x 115.6cm*) sashing strips. Sew 4¼" x WOF (*10.8cm x WOF*) strips together end to end. Cut two 4¼" x 45½" (*10.8cm x 115.6cm*) borders.

3. Assemble quilt top as shown, inserting one 4" x 45½" (*10.2cm x 115.6cm*) sashing strip between each row and adding a 4¼" x 45½" (*10.8cm x 115.6cm*) border strip to the top and bottom. Note that Row 4 has been rotated 180 degrees so that the colored fabric appears on the right.

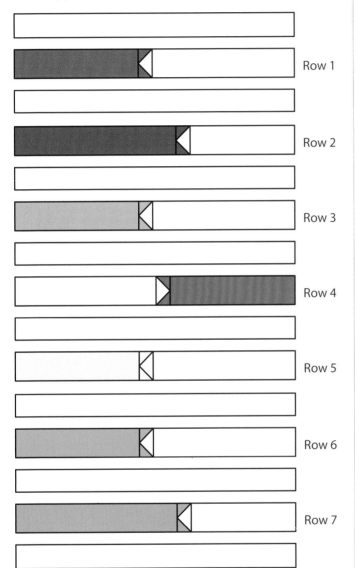

Row 1

Row 2

Row 3

Row 4

Row 5

Row 6

Row 7

FINISHING

See Materials and Cutting sections (page 82) for materials needed for finishing. Cut backing fabric into two equal lengths of 54" x WOF (*137.2cm x WOF*). Trim selvages and sew together along the long sides to make a backing about 54" x 80" (*137.2cm x 203.2cm*). Trim to about 54" x 68" (*137.2cm x 172.7cm*). Finish quilt using Basting (page 17), Quilting (page 18), and Binding (page 19) instructions.

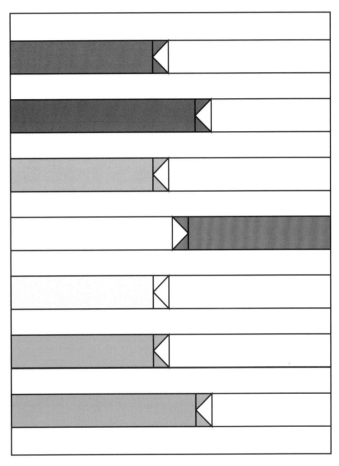

Travel Posts Quilt Top Diagram

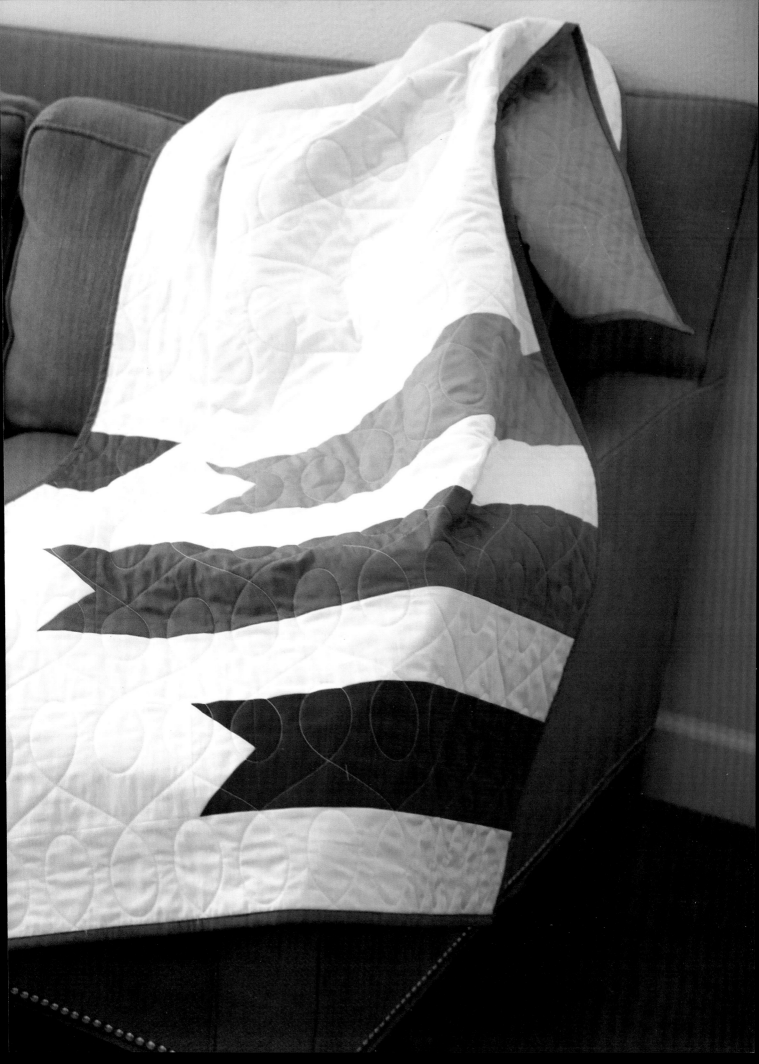

UINTA

The negative space in this design allows a quilter some artistic freedom when it comes to quilting. I decided to use my BabyLock Sashiko sewing machine to achieve a hand-quilted look, but a quilter could really do some fun designs with all that negative space. The + sign would feel heavy if left alone, but the lines even out the weight and allow this quilt to be beautiful and balanced when viewed in any orientation! These simple two tones and designs bring a modern look and feel to this quilt pattern. You can create wall art or a larger size quilt with this pattern.

MATERIALS

Yardage is based on 42" (106.7cm)–wide fabric.

	Wall Art (16" x 19" [40.6cm x 48.3cm])	Baby (30" x 40" [76.2cm x 101.6cm])	Lap (50" x 67" [127cm x 170.2cm])
Fabric A (white)	½ yard (45.7cm)	1¼ yards (114.3cm)	3 yards (274.3cm)
Fabric B (black)	⅛ yard (11.4cm) or one fat eighth	¼ yard (22.9cm)	⅜ yard (34.3cm)
Backing	⅔ yard (61cm)	1⅓ yards (121.9cm)	3¼ yards (297.2cm)
Binding	¼ yard (22.9cm)	⅓ yard (30.5cm)	½ yard (45.7cm)
Batting	⅔ yard (61cm)	1⅓ yards (121.9cm)	3¼ yards (297.2cm)

Finished Sizes:
Wall Art (16" x 19" [*40.6cm x 48.3cm*]),
Baby (30" x 40" [*76.2cm x 101.6cm*]), and
Lap (50" x 67" [*127cm x 170.2cm*])
Skill Level: Beginner
Fabrics Used: Art Gallery Fabrics Pure
Solids in Caviar and Snow

Pieced and quilted by Elizabeth Chappell

CUTTING

All measurements include ¼" (0.5cm) seam allowances.

	Wall Art (16" x 19" [40.6cm x 48.3cm])	Baby (30" x 40" [76.2cm x 101.6cm])	Lap (50" x 67" [127cm x 170.2cm])
Fabric A (white)	One 8½" x WOF (21.6cm x 7.6cm) strip, then subcut: • One 8½" x 16½" (21cm x 41.9cm) rectangle [G] From remainder of 8½" x WOF (21.6cm x WOF) strip, cut: • One 4½" x WOF (11.4cm x WOF) strip, then subcut: • One 4½" x 11½" (11.4cm x 29.2cm) rectangle [D] • One 4½" x 1½" (11.4cm x 3.8cm) rectangle [E] • Four 2" (5 cm) squares [A] • One 3½" x 16" (8.9cm x 40.6cm) rectangle [K] One 1½" x WOF (3.8cm x WOF) strip, then subcut: • Two 1½" x 16½" (3.8cm x 41.9cm) rectangles [F, I] • One 1½" x 8½" (3.8cm x 21.6cm) rectangle [J]	Cut one 18½" x WOF (47cm x WOF) strip, then *subcut:* • One 18½" x 30½" (47cm x 77.5cm) rectangle [G] • Four 3½" (8.9cm) squares [A] One 8½" x WOF (21.6cm x WOF) strip, then *subcut:* • One 8½" x 20½" (21.6cm x 52.1cm) rectangle [D] • One 8½" x 2½" (21.6cm x 6.4cm) rectangle [E] • One 2½" x 15½" (6.4cm x 39.4cm) rectangle [J] One 6" x WOF (15.2cm x WOF) strip, then *subcut:* • One 6" x 30½" (15.2cm x 77.5cm) rectangle [K] One 3" x WOF (7.6cm x WOF) strip, then *subcut:* • One 3" x 30½" (7.6cm x 77.5cm) rectangle [F] Cut one 2½" x WOF (6.4cm x WOF) strip, then *subcut:* • One 2½" x 30½" (6.4cm x 77.5cm) rectangle [I]	Two 30½" x WOF (77.5cm x WOF) strips, then *subcut:* • One 30½" x 40½" (77.5cm x 102.9cm) rectangle [G] • One 30½" x 10½" (77.5cm x 26.7cm) rectangle [G] From remainder of 30½" (77.5cm) strip, cut: • Two 25½" x 9½" (64.8cm x 24.1cm) rectangles [K] • Two 25½" x 4½" (64.8cm x 11.4cm) rectangles [F] One 14" x WOF (35.6cm x WOF) strip, then *subcut:* • One 14" x 32½" (35.6cm x 82.6cm) rectangle [D] One 5½" x WOF (14cm x WOF), then *subcut:* • Four 5½" (14cm) squares [A] • One 5" x 14" (12.7cm x 35.6cm) rectangle [E] Three 4" x WOF (10.2cm x WOF) strips, then *subcut:* • Three 4" x 25½" (10.2cm x 64.8cm) rectangles [I, J]
Fabric B (black)	One 1½" x WOF (3.8cm x WOF) strip, then *subcut:* • One 1½" x 16½" (3.8cm x 41.9cm) rectangle [H] • One 1½" x 8½" (3.8cm x 21.6cm) rectangle [J] • One 1½" x 4½" (3.8cm x 11.4cm) rectangle [C] • Two 1½" x 2" (3.8cm x 5cm) rectangles [B]	Two 2½" x WOF (6.4cm x WOF) strips, then *subcut:* • One 2½" x 30½" (6.4cm x 77.5cm) rectangle [H] • One 2½" x 8½" (6.4cm x 21.6cm) rectangle [C] • One 2½" x 15½" (6.4cm x 39.4cm) rectangle [J] • Two 2½" x 3½" (6.4cm x 8.9cm) rectangles [B]	Three 4" x WOF (10.2cm x WOF) strips, then *subcut:* • One 4" x 40½" (10.2cm x 102.9cm) rectangle [H] • One 4" x 10½" (10.2cm x 26.7cm) rectangle [H] • One 4" x 25½" (10.2cm x 64.8cm) rectangle [J] • One 4" x 14" (10.2cm x 35.6cm) rectangle [C] • Two 4" x 5½" (10.2cm x 14cm) rectangles [B]
Binding	Two 2½" x WOF (6.4cm x WOF) strips	Four 2½" x WOF (6.4cm x WOF) strips	Seven 2½" x WOF (6.4cm x WOF) strips

PIECING

The following instructions make one Wall Art size (16" x 19½" [*40.6cm x 49.5cm*]) quilt top. To make another size quilt top, replace the listed size pieces with the correct sizes for your quilt top, or if you are making the Lap sized quilt (50" x 67" [*127cm x 170.2cm*]) follow piecing instructions on page 92. See the Materials and Cutting charts (pages 88 and 90) to see what pieces to replace.

1. Sew one Fabric A 2" (*5cm*) [A] square RST with one Fabric B 1½" x 2" (*3.8cm x 5cm*) [B] rectangle. Press seam toward Fabric B.

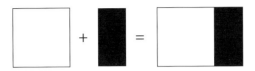

2. Sew one Fabric A 2" (*5cm*) [A] square RST on the opposite side of your Fabric B [B] rectangle. Press seam toward Fabric B.

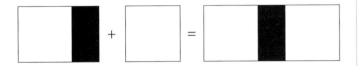

3. Repeat steps 1 and 2 to make two matching rectangle units.

4. Sew one Fabric B 4½" x 1½" (*11.4cm x 3.8cm*) [C] rectangle RST to the top of one rectangle piece from step 3. Press seam toward Fabric B.

5. Sew one rectangle unit from step 3 on the opposite side of your 4½" x 1½" (*11.4cm x 3.8cm*) [C] rectangle. Press seam towards Fabric B. Makes one 4½" (*11.4cm*) cross square.

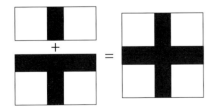

6. Sew one Fabric A 4½" x 11½" (*11.4cm x 29.2cm*) [D] rectangle RST to the right side of the cross square. Press seam toward Fabric A.

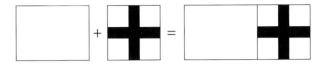

7. Sew one Fabric A 1½" x 4½" (*3.8cm x 11.4cm*) [E] rectangle RST to the left side of the cross square. Press seam towards Fabric A.

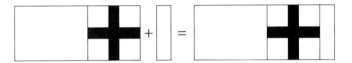

8. Sew one Fabric A 16½" x 1½" (*41.9cm x 3.8cm*) [F] rectangle RST to the top of the unit from step 7. Press fabric toward Fabric A.

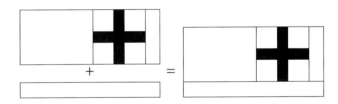

9. Sew one Fabric A 16½" x 8½" (*41.9cm x 21.6cm*) [G] rectangle RST to the bottom of the unit from step 8. Press seam toward Fabric A.

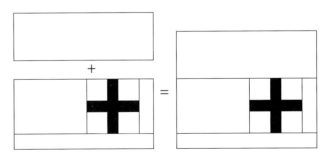

10. Sew one Fabric B 16½" x 1½" (*41.9cm x 3.8cm*) [H] rectangle RST to the bottom of the unit from step 9. Press seam toward Fabric B.

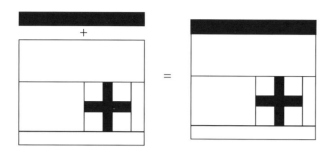

11. Sew one Fabric A 16½" x 1½" (*41.9cm x 3.8cm*) [I] rectangle RST to the bottom of the unit from step 10. Press seam toward Fabric B.

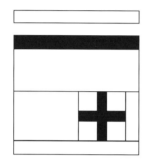

12. Sew one Fabric A 8½" x 1½" (*21.6cm x 3.8cm*) [J] rectangle and one Fabric B 8½" x 1½" (*21.6cm x 3.8cm*) [J] rectangle RST on the short side. Press seam toward Fabric B.

13. Sew your Fabric A and Fabric B unit from step 12 RST to the bottom of the unit from step 11. Press seam in one direction.

14. Sew one Fabric A 16½" x 3½" (*41.9cm x 8.9cm*) [K] rectangle to the bottom of the unit from step 13. Press seam toward Fabric A.

PIECING FOR LAP SIZE QUILT ONLY

From Fabric A

1. Gather the Fabric A 30½" x 40½" (*77.5cm x 102.9cm*) rectangle and 30½" x 10½" (*77.5cm x 102.9cm*) rectangle. Sew RST along the 30½" (*77.5cm*) side to make one 30½" x 50½" (*77.5cm x 128.3cm*) rectangle [G].

2. Gather two Fabric A 25½" x 9½" (*64.8cm x 24.1cm*) rectangles and sew RST along the 9½" (*24.1cm*) sides to make one 50½" x 9½" (*128.3cm x 24.1cm*) rectangle [K].

3. Gather two Fabric A 25½" x 4½" (*64.8cm x 11.4cm*) rectangles and sew RST along the 4½" (*11.4cm*) sides to make one 50½" x 4 ½" (*128.3cm x 11.4cm*) rectangle [F].

4. Gather two Fabric A 25½" x 4" (*64.8cm x 10.2cm*) rectangles and sew RST along the 4" (*10.2cm*) to make one 50½" x 4" (*128.3cm x 10.2cm*) rectangle [I].

From Fabric B

5. Gather the Fabric B 4" x 40½" (*10.2cm x 102.9cm*) and rectangle 4" x 10½" (*10.2cm x 102.9cm*) rectangle. Sew RST along the 4" (*10.2cm*) sides to make one 50½" x 4" (*128.3cm x 10.2cm*) rectangle [H].

FINISHING

See Materials and Cutting sections (pages 88 and 90) for materials needed for finishing. Follow Basting (page 17), Quilting (page 18), and Binding (page 19) instructions to finish your quilt.

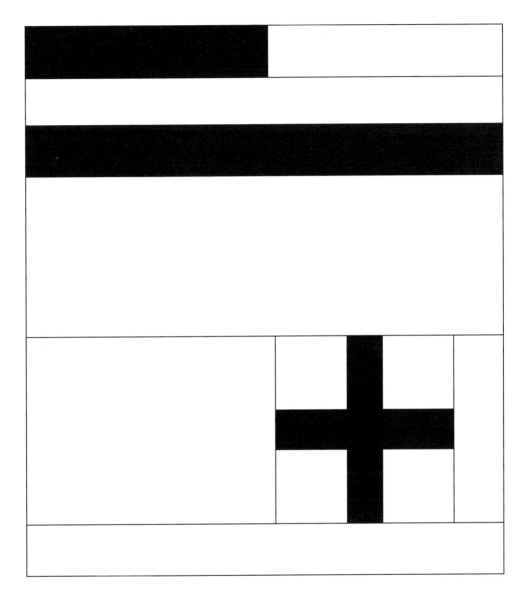

Uinta Quilt Top Diagram

About the Author

Born in Minnesota, Elizabeth Chappell was introduced to quilting at a young age through her mother but didn't become interested in the craft herself until much later in life. In 2015, she attended the Houston Quilt Market, and the rest was history!

At the same time Elizabeth was learning to quilt, she and her friend started a monthly subscription box for quilters that offered the best quilt patterns and notions they could find. During her search for each box, she was inspired to begin designing and writing quilt patterns of her own.

Today, Elizabeth lives outside of Houston, Texas, and is a talented quilter, pattern designer, and owner of Quilters Candy, where she sells her patterns, offers instructional courses, and hosts an online membership guild. Additionally, she has also started a podcast called Craft to Career, where she has insightful discussions with other creatives, makers, and entrepreneurs on how to turn your talents into a successful career!

To learn more about Elizabeth and see her work, visit *www.QuiltersCandy.com* or find her on Facebook (@QuiltersCandyBox), Instagram (@Quilters_Candy and @QuiltersCandyMembership), and YouTube (Elizabeth Chappell).

Acknowledgments

I am forever grateful to my mom, who, despite me not being interested in quilting until I was in my 30s, instilled a love of quilting, fabric, and beauty.

Thank you to my husband, Brad, for supporting me as I dream. Thanks for letting me stay up way too late sewing and working and for being my go-to for business and quilting conversations. You've always believed in me, sometimes even more than I have.

Thank you to Tracey Berrett. You have been a dear friend to me, who I will always cherish. The cherry on top is that you got me to become a quilter!

Thank you to my friend and mentor, Cheryl Tessitore. She has been a guide, teacher, and wonderful friend to me from the beginning. Thank you, Cheryl!

Thank you to my kids for being patient and supportive and not throwing a fit while I juggled a million things. Thank you for not just being okay with but being excited for me as I reach my dreams.

Thank you to Jamie McPheeters for helping me make these quilts on time. You have been a supportive friend and colleague.

Thank you to Jill Coterie, a talented long arm quilter who I can trust to run free with any of my quilts.

Thank you to Sarah Nielsen. You are one talented painter, artist, and a wonderful friend. Thank you for countless hours of chatting with me over color theory and painting the lovely paintings in this book.

Index